THE WORLD'S GREAT
AIRCRAFT
CARRIERS

FROM THE CIVIL WAR TO THE PRESENT

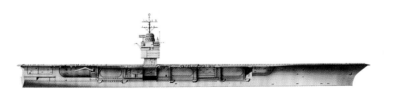

THE WORLD'S GREAT
AIRCRAFT CARRIERS

FROM THE CIVIL WAR TO THE PRESENT
ANTONY PRESTON

THUNDER BAY
P·R·E·S·S

Copyright © 1999 Amber Books Ltd

This edition published in 2000 by
Thunder Bay Press
An imprint of the Advantage Publishers Group
5880 Oberlin Drive
San Diego, CA 92121–4794
www.advantagebooksonline.com

ISBN 1-57145-261-3

Library of Congress Cataloging-in-Publication Data
available upon request

Editor: Matthew Tanner
Design: Double Elephant /Rita Wüthrich
Picture Research: Ken Botham

Printed in The Slovak Republic

Contents

CHAPTER ONE

Pioneering Days

In the nineteenth century all the world's imperial navies realised the
potential of having airborne lookouts to provide long-range reconnaissance
for their fleets. However, there were drawbacks to kites and balloons,
and the first flying machines proved totally unsuitable for taking off
from a ship, much less land on one. But Britain and the United States
persevered, and the first true aircraft carriers were born.

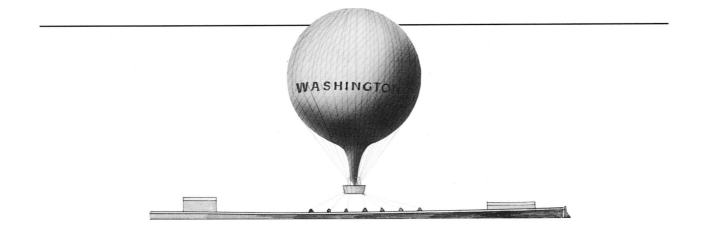

The aircraft carrier is an anomalous creation, combining vulnerability with great fighting power. Its
rise to pre-eminence has been rapid; as late as 1939
many naval planners regarded it as an ancillary to the
battleship, and despite periodic questions about its
effectiveness, 60 years later it is the most powerful
warship in existence. Yet, when manned flight first
became practicable it is astonishing to read how soon
the potential of 'air-capable' ships was realised.

Balloons became popular towards the end of the
eighteenth century, but the first suggestion of a naval
application came from Rear Admiral Henry Knowles
of the Royal Navy in 1803. It was his proposal that
a frigate should be converted to operate a balloon, to

Left: Daredevil pilot Eugene B. Ely landing on the stern
platform of the armoured cruiser USS *Pennsylvania* on
18 January 1911.

reconnoitre Brest harbour. In 1818 another
Englishman, Charles Rogier, outlined a ship fitted to
operate free-floating balloons armed with clockwork-
fused bombs, to attack an enemy fleet in harbour. In
1846 John Wise proposed a tethered balloon, for dropping explosives on Vera Cruz during the Mexican-
American War, for use on land or from a ship at sea.
However, the first use of balloons in war did not occur
until 1849, when the Austrians were besieging Venice.
The plan was to use small, free-floating hot-air balloons to drop explosives on the city. Most of these
attacks were mounted from land, but on 12 July 1849
a number were released from the steamer *Volcano*.

This attack proved totally unsuccessful and left
unmanned balloons out of favour until the late 1880s,
when Frederick Gower tried to persuade the Admiralty
to build a ship to operate 'aerial batteries'. His idea
came to nothing, but interest in manned captive

7

balloons at sea surfaced again during the American Civil War. The Union Army began using balloons on an *ad hoc* basis, and on 3 August 1861 John La Mountain made ascents from the deck of the army transport *Fanny*, a converted tug. There are unsubstantiated claims that La Mountain made another flight from the steamer *Adriatic*, but there can be little doubt that these were the first manned balloon flights from a ship. The Union Balloon Corps operated a number of reconnaissance balloons, and in August 1861 acquired a coal barge from the Washington Navy Yard for conversion. Named *George Washington Parke Custis*, she was the first craft configured solely for aerial duties. She was returned to the Navy Yard in 1863, but her balloon flew from the Army gunboat *Mayflower* in mid-1863. Another balloon was used to direct Union ships' gunfire on the Mississippi in 1862; a role which was to be resurrected half a century later.

THE SAUSAGE-SHAPED BALLOON

By the 1890s interest in balloons was reviving. This was largely because the range of guns was increasing beyond the horizon of a masthead observer and greater visibility was required. Experiments aboard the French battleship *Formidable* showed that a balloon's observer could see as much as 40km (25 miles) further than an observer in a ship.

Below: The coal barge *George Washington Parke Custis* (1861) was the first ever craft configured solely to operate aerial vehicles.

The new science of aeronautical engineering was also making its presence felt. For more than a century balloons had been spherical or pear-shaped, but the German sausage-shaped kite balloon used a series of fins and vents to keep it stable in all but the strongest winds. Observers must have been delighted, as the motion of spherical balloons was frequently so violent as to incapacitate the occupants of the basket.

Germany tried to keep the 'secret' of the kite balloon to itself, but this did not prevent the Royal Swedish Navy from adopting it and acquiring the first 'aviation vessel' in Europe in 1904. The Balloon Depot Ship No.1 (*Ballondepotfartyg Nr. 1*) was a 244-tonne (220-ton) unpowered barge, reminiscent of the *George Washington Parke Custis*, but unlike her, designed and built for the purpose. She was relegated to coast defence in 1915, but was deployed in the annual manoeuvres until 1929, when she was sold. The French converted the old torpedo-boat carrier *Foudre* to operate balloons for the annual manoeuvres of 1898 and 1901, but the risk inherent in using hydrogen led the Navy to the conclusion that kites capable of lifting a man offered more potential.

PORT ARTHUR – A MINOR LANDMARK

The Imperial Russian Navy was very interested in kites and balloons, but they contributed little or nothing in the war against Japan in 1904-5. It was left to the Japanese land forces to show what could be done. On 9 August 1905, during the siege of Port Arthur, the commander of the Japanese siege artillery went aloft

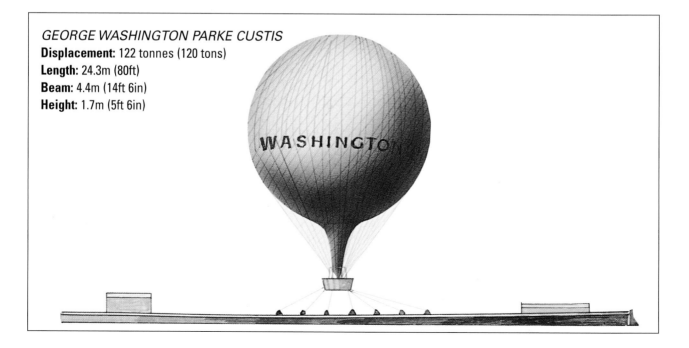

GEORGE WASHINGTON PARKE CUSTIS
Displacement: 122 tonnes (120 tons)
Length: 24.3m (80ft)
Beam: 4.4m (14ft 6in)
Height: 1.7m (5ft 6in)

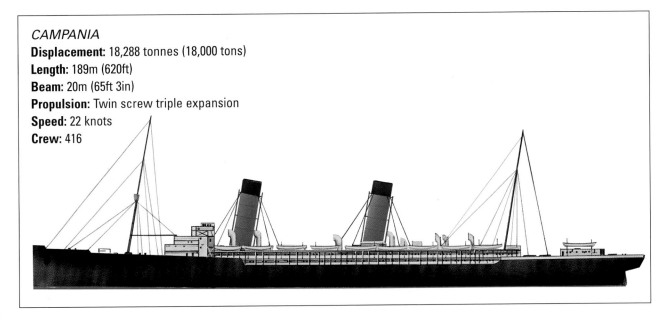

CAMPANIA
Displacement: 18,288 tonnes (18,000 tons)
Length: 189m (620ft)
Beam: 20m (65ft 3in)
Propulsion: Twin screw triple expansion
Speed: 22 knots
Crew: 416

to direct the fire of two 120mm (4.7in) guns against Russian warships in the harbour. One battleship was slightly damaged and another was hit 10 times. A lighter moored alongside was sunk, leaving her captain wounded and three sailors killed. At Vladivostok an army engineer, Captain Fyodor Postnikov, operated a series of spherical and kite balloons to try to spot Japanese sea mines. He began by using a steam cutter but went on to convert four transports and the armoured cruiser *Rossia*, and by the end of the war had nearly 100 personnel from the Army and Navy. Attempts to direct the *Rossia*'s gunnery against land targets were inconclusive, and an attempt to use her balloon to find Japanese shipping during a raid into the Yellow Sea in May 1905 was marred by technical failure. It was, however, a minor landmark in naval history – the first operational use of a balloon at sea during hostilities.

MAN-LIFTING KITES

Back in the Baltic, the Russian Navy was working on the conversion of the first self-propelled seagoing aviation vessel. An elderly former North German liner, the *Lahn*, was purchased and renamed *Russ*. Reclassified as a second-class cruiser, she was converted at Libau in 1904-5, while Russia was at war with Japan, with the after part of the ship gutted to accommodate gas generators, auxiliary engines, dynamos and winches. Unfortunately her hull was so decrepit that she proved unseaworthy, but her crew were spared the horror of the disastrous Battle of Tsushima, as Admiral Nebogatov sent her back to Libau from the Skagerrak.

Above: The old Cunard Blue Riband winner *Campania* was converted to a seaplane carrier in 1914-15, with a platform over her forecastle.

AN ITALIAN FIRST

The Italians installed a spherical balloon in the cruiser *Elba*, but replaced it with a kite balloon for the 1907 manoeuvres off Sicily. Her sister ship, *Liguria*, also operated a kite balloon in 1908-11, while the *Elba* was converted to a seaplane tender in 1914. During the war against Turkey in 1911-12 the Italians used aircraft, airships and balloons, pioneering virtually all the early applications, and in particular spotting for artillery. The Italian Navy was very anxious to enjoy these advantages, and the brigantine *Cavalmarino* was converted to a balloon ship at Tripoli at the end of 1911. In November or December 1911 the kite balloon spotted fall of shot for the battleship *Re Umberto* and the cruiser *Carlo Alberto*, the first time since 1862 that a lighter-than-air machine had guided warship gunfire on active service.

In parallel with ballooning, the kite seemed to offer similar promise. Its relevance to naval use was recognised as early as 1806, when Lord Cochrane flew kites from the frigate HMS *Pallas* to drop propaganda leaflets along the shores of the Bay of Biscay. Nearly half a century later his son Admiral Sir Charles Cochrane devised and tested a means of towing 'torpedoes' (casks filled with gunpowder). It was feasible, but never used in action, and thereafter interest lapsed. Not until the Australian Lawrence Hargrave invented the box kite

FOUDRE
Displacement: 6186 tonnes (6089 tons)
Length: 118.7m (389ft 5in)
Beam: 17.2m (56ft 5in)
Height: 7.2m (23ft 7in)
Propulsion: Twin screw triple expansion
Speed: 19 knots
Armament: Eight 9.9cm (3.9in) guns
Crew: 328
Aircraft: Four

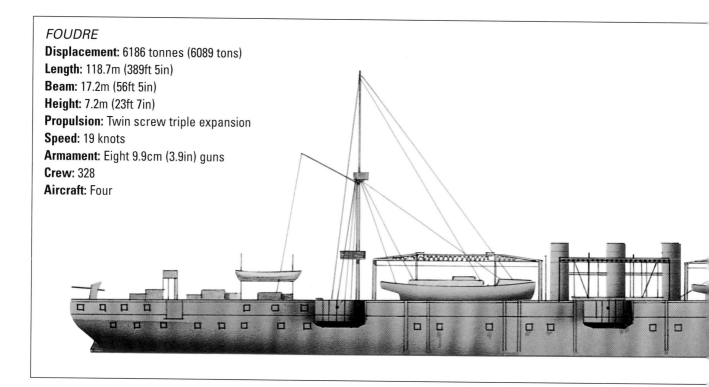

Above: The *Foudre* was built as a French depot ship for 10 small torpedo boats. She was later converted to a seaplane carrier, in which role she served in World War I.

Below: The Italian Navy's converted seaplane carrier *Europa* served in the Adriatic from 1915 to 1918. She operated eight aircraft.

EUROPA
Displacement: 8945 tonnes (8805 tons)
Length: 123m (403ft)
Beam: 14m (46ft)
Height: 7.6m (25ft)
Propulsion: Single screw, vertical triple expansion
Speed: 12 knots
Armament: Two 30mm (1.2in) anti-aircraft guns
Crew: 394
Aircraft: Eight

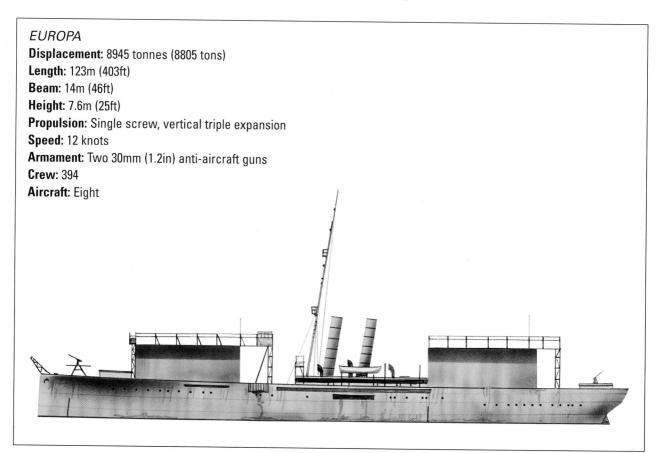

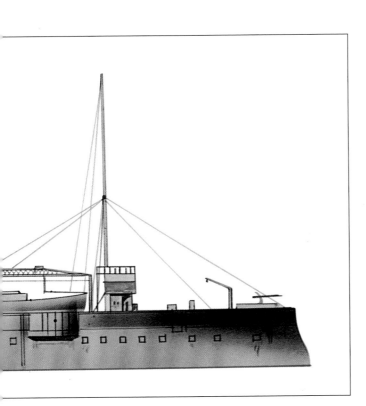

the big cruiser HMS *Good Hope* and the second-class cruiser HMS *Doris*. A more exhaustive series of trials started in 1907, but at the end of 1908 Cody was officially informed that 'Their Lordships' had no intention of bringing man-lifting kites into service. It was Cody's misfortune to have arrived on the scene just at the moment when powered aircraft were becoming feasible.

The US Navy also investigated man-lifting kites in 1911, using kites designed by Samuel F. Perkins. The ship selected was the armoured cruiser USS *Pennsylvania*, which had already been used for the first landing by a powered aircraft (see below). The trials took place on 24 January 1911 in the Santa Barbara Channel off the coast of Southern California, and although successful, were not followed up. The French Navy also tested kites in 1911, aboard the armoured cruiser *Edgar Quinet* in August that year. The designer was the Army engineer Captain Jacques Saccony whose kites were similar to Cody's. He too received little more than a sympathetic hearing, and his system was not adopted.

However exciting these developments might have been at the time, they lacked the flexibility of powered flight, and it is not difficult to see why navies became more interested in aircraft at this stage. Certainly, when Clement Ader published his book *l'Aviation Militaire* in 1909 he wrote of the indispensable need for a ship capable of operating powered aircraft, rather than balloons or kites. He predicted not only the take-off and landing of aircraft but also the need for a wide, clear deck, deck-lifts, 'island' superstructures offset to one side, hangars to protect aircraft from the weather, and the necessity for a good turn of speed

POWERING UP

Unfortunately the crude aircraft of the day could barely take-off from a ship, let alone land on one. If such perilous operations were contemplated, the aviators wanted the ship to be at anchor or moving very slowly to avoid wind eddies. Ader's prophetic ideas were ignored by the French military for another 10 years, leaving Great Britain and the United States to make all the running. But in the early years of the twentieth century the rapid development of powered heavier-than-air craft overtook ballooning as the most promising line of development. There was enormous interest in aviation in Great Britain, France, Germany and the United States, and the British, possessing the largest navy in the world, wanted to keep abreast of all developments.

in the early 1890s did interest in kites reawaken. It was capable of lifting a man, and proved aerodynamically stable and even steerable. It was, in fact, a sophisticated machine, needing only the addition of power to make the transition to the aircraft as we know it.

BRITISH AND AMERICAN TESTS

British Army experiments started under Captain Baden-Powell of the Scots Guards (older brother of the founder of the Scouts Association). With the encouragement of Commander Reginald Tupper RN, he carried out trials with the Navy as well. The trials involved passing dispatches from the destroyer HMS *Daring* to a lightship, but the Admiralty showed no interest in any further trials. The American Samuel Cody started experiments with man-lifting kites in England around 1900, and when he wrote to the Admiralty in February 1903 offering to demonstrate his kites he received a sympathetic hearing from Tupper, now a captain. The Royal Navy was principally interested in kites as a means of extending radio aerials to increase range, and Tupper reported enthusiastically.

In April 1903 flights were achieved from the old ironclad HMS *Hector* and the destroyer HMS *Starfish*. Despite scepticism and downright obstruction from some quarters, kite systems were fitted in the battleships HMS *Majestic* and HMS *Revenge*,

AN EARLY REQUIREMENT

The naval requirement to get ships to sea stemmed from one basic need which had been valid since the days of Drake and Nelson: reconnaissance. There is a practical limit to visibility with the naked eye, and even the most eagle-eyed lookout, posted at the tallest masthead, equipped with the most powerful telescope or binoculars, could not hope to see more than 65km (40 miles) in ideal conditions. Providing the vital information about enemy movements, scouting cruisers had to be stationed in patrol lines, near enough to remain in visual contact with each other to be able to exchange signals. The invention of radio at the beginning of the century reduced the dependence on visual signalling, but an individual ship could not hope to see anything outside her limit of visibility.

In 1908 the US Navy decided to launch an aircraft from one of its battleships, but nothing happened until 1910 because the Navy owned no aircraft.

The decision was prompted by the news that a Hamburg-America liner would fly an aircraft off a platform on her foredeck, to speed up deliveries of mail to New York. International tension was rising, and the Navy suspected that the German military were using the mail service as a cover for testing new ways of attacking America. Accordingly, on 9 November 1910 the new light cruiser USS *Birmingham* was earmarked for installation of a platform over her bows.

Captain Chambers, the officer in charge of the experiment, had more trouble finding a pilot than a ship, and after interviewing Wilbur Wright and several others, he met an exhibition stunt pilot working with the flying boat pioneer Glenn Curtiss. He was Eugene B. Ely, and he accepted the challenge with enthusiasm. Speed was now paramount, because the Hamburg-America liner was about to carry out a similar experiment, also using an American pilot. Norfolk Navy Yard worked over the weekend to finish the 25m x 7m

(83ft x 24ft) platform, and on 14 November 1910 Ely's pusher biplane took off from the *Birmingham* and vanished into the mist, to land about two-and-a-half miles away in Chesapeake Bay.

ELY MAKES HISTORY

The next step was even more ambitious. The big armoured cruiser USS *Pennsylvania* was fitted with a sloping landing deck nearly 37m (120ft) long and over 9m (29ft) wide, built over her stern to allow Ely to touch down while the ship was steaming slowly into the wind. To help the aircraft to slow down, a series of 22 transverse wires weighted by sandbags were provided. On 18 January 1911 the weather was poor and the *Pennsylvania*'s captain decided that he had too little room to manoeuvre, and insisted on remaining at anchor. As a result the wind was blowing from astern, the worst combination for any pilot. In spite of the difficulties, Ely succeeded in putting his aircraft down. He pulled his aircraft up just short of the

Above: HMS *Ben-my-Chree* was one of three Isle of Man steamers converted to seaplane carriers in 1915. One of her Short 184s torpedoed a Turkish transport.

'round down', cut his engine and allowed the tail wind to carry him over 11 of the wires. He stopped in under 10m (33ft).

After such a brilliant success the US Navy decided to take stock. It would be a long time before sufficient pilots could be trained and suitable aircraft could be bought. Contemporary aircraft lacked any means of communicating with a parent ship or shore station, and lacked any weapon more powerful than a hand grenade, so there was no immediate tactical role for them. Inevitably, interest now switched to seaplanes (also known as floatplanes or hydro-aeroplanes), either specially designed types or standard land aircraft fitted with flotation bags. The leading designer, Glenn Curtiss, showed in February 1911 that a floatplane could be launched from a ship (the *Pennsylvania* was used once again), then land alongside its parent ship and be hoisted back on board. In April 1914 the United States was embroiled in a dispute with Mexico, and the Navy sent six of its twelve floatplanes to Vera Cruz on board the battleship *Mississippi*. These provided valuable scouting for the landing parties, and though one sustained some damage from rifle fire, it returned safely.

The Royal Navy was also showing great enthusiasm for naval aviation. Early in 1909 funds were allocated for the construction of a rigid airship, the Mayfly. The reason for this bias was the German Navy's interest in Count Zeppelin's large dirigible airships, but British efforts were soon redirected. In September 1911 the Mayfly was wrecked while leaving her hangar for a maiden flight, resulting in the break up of the Navy's Airship Section. But five officers were given permission to undergo training as pilots, and two more learned to fly at their own expense.

BRITISH TAKE-OFF

Commander Oliver Schwann RN made the first ever British waterborne take-off on 18 November 1911, but he crashed while trying to land on water. Two weeks later Lieutenant Arthur Longmore RN succeeded in landing a Short S.27. Lieutenant Charles Sampson RN was keen to emulate Ely's feats and on 10 January 1912 he flew off a platform over the forecastle of the battleship HMS *Africa*. Four months later he repeated the take-off, but this time from the battleships HMS *Hibernia* and HMS *London* during a review in Weymouth Bay. May 1912 saw an even more important step, when the Committee of Imperial Defence called for the establishment of an aviation service. Two wings of this Royal Flying Corps (RFC) were to share responsibility for land and sea operations, but in 1914 the naval wing's widely differing role was recognised by renaming it the Royal Naval Air Service (RNAS).

WHAT'S IN A NAME?

At the end of 1912 the Admiralty ordered the old light cruiser HMS *Hermes* to be converted to a 'parent ship' for naval aircraft, with a flying-off deck over the forecastle and a stowage deck over the stern. One of the first experiments was to embark an aircraft with folding wings, a portent of the future. Winston Churchill, the new First Lord of the Admiralty, disliked the clumsy term 'hydro-aeroplane', and

insisted on 'seaplane' becoming the official description. HMS *Hermes* carried out numerous experiments, including trials of French aircraft, and took part in the annual manoeuvres in 1913. She proved so successful that a mercantile hull was bought for conversion to a seaplane carrier.

The new ship proved to be very well thought out, with a launching system using light wheeled trolleys which were jettisoned after the seaplane was airborne. She would also have a proper hold, workshops and heavy cranes to lift seaplanes in and out. The choice of name by Winston Churchill was unusual, in that it had not been used since 1588, but it proved an inspired choice: *Ark Royal*.

TENSION RISES

The Germans' predilection for large airships has already been mentioned. On the plus side they offered a much greater range as well as the the priceless military asset of a relatively large bomb load, but their sheer size , not to mention their instability, especially in high winds, militated against flights from ships. The Italians embarked a seaplane on the battleship *Dante Alighieri* in 1913 but failed to develop the idea. The French, on the other hand, were very keen, and converted the *Foudre* to operate seaplanes. Commissioned in 1912, she took part in the 1913 manoeuvres. The Japanese followed a similar route, converting a merchant ship, the SS *Wakamiya*, at the end of 1913 to

Above: Squadron Commander Dunning's Sopwith Pup stacks during this third attempt to land on the forecastle of HMS *Furious* in August 1917.

carry two seaplanes along with disassembled components for a second pair.

Alongside these early developments in carrier technology was the inescapable fact that tension in Europe was rising. In the final few months of peace before the outbreak of World War I, the leading navies showed their intention to use aircraft as weapons of war, rather than technical curiosities. Under the stimulus of war, progress would now accelerate very rapidly, albeit not very smoothly.

CHAPTER TWO

Naval Aviation Goes to War

The outbreak of World War I gave an impetus to the design and development of the aircraft carrier. The Royal Navy converted a number of liners and steamers to be aircraft carriers, but during the war dedicated carriers were built, such as the *Argus* and *Hermes*, which was the first warship in the world designed to operate with conventional aircraft. In addition, the Americans continued with their carrier research.

The outbreak of war in August 1914 saw the dispatch of nearly all the British Army's aircraft to France, followed shortly afterwards by a squadron of six RNAS seaplanes to Dunkirk, under the command of Squadron Commander Sampson. This left Britain with no air defence, and the task was transferred to the RNAS. But as the Germans had no short-term plans to bomb Britain, the naval pilots were virtually free to develop ideas for co-operation with the Fleet.

Left: HMS *Hermes*, laid down in 1918 and completed in 1925, was the world's first warship designed to operate conventional (wheeled) aircraft.

HMS *Ark Royal* was not yet ready so the Admiralty requisitioned three cross-Channel steamers, the SS *Empress*, SS *Engadine* and SS *Riviera* for conversion to seaplane carriers. They were fast, an important requirement, and with their promenade and boat decks cleared there was room for a canvas hangar, large enough to house four seaplanes. The principal drawback was their short range, but the arrangement for hoisting seaplanes in and out also proved much too cumbersome if the seaplane carrier was in close proximity to hostile forces. Despite these faults the ships were used to launch the first carrier air raid in history, an attack on the Zeppelin base at Cuxhaven

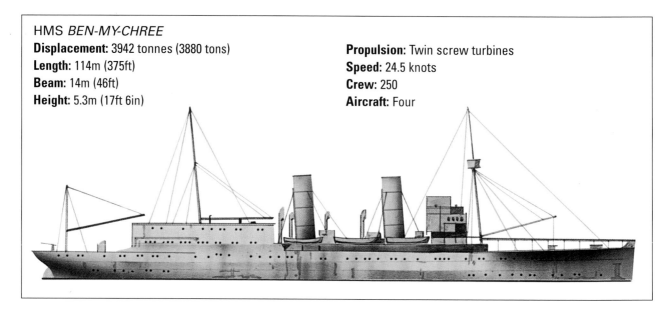

HMS *BEN-MY-CHREE*
Displacement: 3942 tonnes (3880 tons)
Length: 114m (375ft)
Beam: 14m (46ft)
Height: 5.3m (17ft 6in)

Propulsion: Twin screw turbines
Speed: 24.5 knots
Crew: 250
Aircraft: Four

Above: HMS *Ben-my-Chree*, *Manxman* and *Vindex* differed from most earlier conversions in having flying-off decks forward.

on Christmas Day, 1914. RNAS aircraft based in Belgium had already bombed the Zeppelin sheds at Dusseldorf, Tondern and Friedrichshafen. Cuxhaven had been targeted on 25 October but the sea had proved too rough for the seaplanes to take off. The Christmas Day raid was escorted by the Harwich Force of light cruisers and destroyers. Seven out of the nine seaplanes succeeded in becoming airborne; only three returned to the carriers. The raid itself was not a success; target-identification was still in its infancy, and the base was not knocked out. Nevertheless, the potential was there and in response to demands from the Commander-in-Chief of the Grand Fleet a larger, faster hull was sought. The old record-breaking Cunard liner *Campania* was laid up awaiting a last trip to the scrapyard. She was both large and fast enough to keep up with the Fleet, and carried sufficient coal to cross the Atlantic.

THE FIRST FLEET CARRIER

The liner was stripped down to the upper deck, and a ramp was built over the forecastle to allow seaplanes to be launched. When she joined the Grand Fleet in April 1915 she had a nominal capacity of 10-11 aircraft and stowage for eight 35.6cm (14in) torpedoes. Later the forefunnel was replaced by twin uptakes to allow the runway to be extended and the downward angle to be increased. Although HMS *Campania*'s antiquated machinery was always a worry, she met

the basic need for a ship capable of accompanying the Fleet, and as such she was the first 'fleet carrier'. To deal with the scouting Zeppelins, fighters were needed, because they were faster and could climb higher than the heavy seaplanes. Initially the ship carried Sopwith Schneider single-seater scouts and Short 184 seaplanes, and later two-seater Sopwith Strutter reconnaissance aircraft.

The Admiralty pressed ahead with more seaplane conversions, using three Isle of Man steamers with higher endurance, HMS *Ben-my-Chree*, HMS *Manxman* and HMS *Vindex*. HMS *Ark Royal* also joined the Fleet, but she was sent to the Mediterranean for the Dardanelles expedition, where her eight seaplanes flew reconnaissance missions and spotted for bombarding warships. Although she proved well-designed for her role she was very slow, and in mid-1915 was relieved by the 24-knot *Ben-my-Chree*. She made history on 12 August 1915, when one of her Short 184 seaplanes torpedoed a large Turkish transport in the Sea of Marmora. Five days later a pair of seaplanes sank a supply ship and a tug, the latter while the seaplane was taxiing on the surface.

To support the *Ben-my-Chree*, two German prizes, the *Anne* and *Raven II* were converted to carry seaplanes. This small 'task group' under the command of Wing Commander Sampson operated in the Eastern Mediterranean and the Red Sea, harrying Turkish lines of communication. In 1915 she had attacked Turkish shipping in the Sea of Marmora to reduce the flow of supplies to the defenders of the Gallipoli peninsula, and when that campaign was finished was used in a number of other areas. The *Ben-my-Chree* was eventually sunk by Turkish shore batteries off Castelorizo Island in 1917. In January 1918 the Turkish battlecruiser *Yavuz,* which as the German *Goeben* had played a major role in bringing Turkey into the war in August 1914, ran aground off the Dardanelles after a successful sortie. To attack such a tempting target was an opportunity not to be missed, and the *Ark Royal* and *Manxman* were ordered to disable her. But in spite of dropping the unheard-of total of 15.24 tonnes (15 tons) of ordnance, the 29.5kg (65lb) and 51kg (112lb) bombs were too puny. The only alternative was to torpedo her, but the 35.6cm (14in) torpedo was known to be far too light to do any significant damage, and the 45.7cm (18in) proved too heavy. Despite repeated efforts, the seaplanes could not get airborne with the 454kg (1000lb) weapon slung underneath. In the words of the British history of the air:

'Unhappily, the torpedo-loaded Short 184 seaplane could only be made to get off the water and fly under ideal conditions. A calm sea with a light breeze was essential and the engine had to be running perfectly. Further, the weight of the torpedo so restricted the amount of petrol which could be carried that a flight of much more than three-quarters of an hour was not possible. So it came about that while a number of torpedo attacks from the air were attempted, only three were successfully concluded.'

The Italian Navy's principal theatre of operations was the Adriatic, easily patrolled by land-based aircraft, but so air-minded a navy was hardly likely to ignore the potential of ships as a means of moving aircraft long distances at minimum risk. The prolonged battles on the Piave and Isonzo fronts generated a requirement for balloons to spot for long-range artillery, both naval and land-based. In 1916 two armed balloon lighters, the *Luigi Mina* and *Umberto Missana* were converted. A more ambitious project was the conversion of the 6500-tonne (6400-ton) merchant ship SS *Quarto* to a seaplane transport in 1915. Commissioned as the *Europa* in October 1915, she carried eight seaplanes (two reconnaissance type and six fighters). She had two large hangars forward and aft, and could steam at a theoretical maximum of 12 knots. She was stationed at Brindisi in 1915-16 and then in Valona in 1917-18.

The Imperial Russian Navy was anxious to build on its experience with balloon-carriers, and in 1913 bought the 3860-tonne (3800-ton) merchant ship *Imperatritsa Alexandra* for conversion to a seaplane carrier. She was commissioned in February 1915 as

the *Orlitsa* for service in the Baltic, carrying four seaplanes in two hangars, plus a fifth in the hold. She saw action in Courland and the Gulf of Finland in 1916 but was laid up at the time of the Revolution in 1917, and was returned to mercantile service in 1923.

The Black Sea Fleet bought two large cargo liners from Britain in 1913 for conversion to 'aviation cruisers'. Conversion started in 1914 and the *Imperator Alexander I* and *Imperator Nikolai I* joined the fleet at the end of November 1915. They were fitted with a large forward hangar and a flight deck aft, with a capacity for six to eight seaplanes. In February 1916 both took part in a raid on the Turkish coal-shipping port of Zonguldak on the southern shore of the Black Sea. After a bombardment by warships the carriers' planes (probably Grigorovich flying boats) dropped 38 bombs on the harbour, sinking the German coaster *Irmingard*. She was to be the largest merchant ship sunk by air attack during the First World War. Three more 'aviation cruisers' were acquired by the Black Sea Fleet in 1916, the *Dakia, Imperator Trajan* and *Rumynia,* 4572-tonne (4500-ton) merchantmen lent by the Romanian Government for conversion. All three were captured by Germany at Sevastopol and Novorossiisk in April 1918. At the armistice they fell into Allied hands, and were returned to their owners.

MENACING ZEPPELINS

Back in the North Sea, naval aviation was also making rapid progress. The ubiquitous Zeppelins were a serious nuisance, bombing civilian targets and giving away the whereabouts of the Grand Fleet when it was trying to bring the German High Seas Fleet to action.

The first attempt to deal with the 'Zeppelin menace' was made by Commodore Tyrwhitt's Harwich Force, comprising light cruisers and destroyers based on the east coast of England. Early in 1915 a number of the cruisers were fitted with a ramp over the forward 15.25cm (6in) gun to allow a French Deperdussin monoplane fighter to take off. The experiment failed because the tiny monoplane could not gain height fast enough to intercept the Zeppelin, and at maximum altitude its engine became very inefficient. Incendiary ammunition had been developed for use against observation balloons on the Western Front, but until high-performance aircraft could be flown off ships there was little hope of destroying a Zeppelin.

On 3 November 1915 a Bristol C-type Scout was fitted with flotation bags and flown off HMS *Vindex,* the first take-off by a wheeled fighter off the deck of a carrier. This proved to be a false dawn. On 4 May

Above: HMS *Argus* in her dazzle camouflage-scheme just before the armistice in November 1918. Her appearance gave rise to the nickname 'The Flying Island'.

1916 the *Vindex* and *Engadine* launched 11 seaplanes against the Zeppelin sheds at Tondern. Once more a series of minor mishaps spoiled the operation and only one seaplane reached the target, only to find the sheds hidden in mist. Later that month, an even more frustrating series of mishaps prevented the *Engadine* and *Campania* from playing a major role in the Battle of Jutland, when the Grand Fleet finally caught the High Seas Fleet.

HMS *Campania* was attached to the main battle-fleet, while the slower *Engadine* served with the battlecruiser force. Although HMS *Engadine* put to sea as planned, when the Grand Fleet left its anchorage at Scapa Flow on the evening of 30 May the *Campania* did not receive the signal to weigh anchor, and remained tucked away in her remote berth on the north side of the Flow. When she finally got to sea next day she was too far behind to catch up. HMS *Engadine* performed her tasks as ordered, and got one of her Short 184 seaplanes aloft in the afternoon. Flight Lieutenant Rutland and his observer sent three sighting reports back but the *Engadine*'s radio equipment took so long to get the information to the flagship HMS *Lion* that the staff dismissed her reports.

Though Jutland brought many recriminations in its wake, an important staff conference, held at Longhope in the Orkneys towards the end of 1916, reached the conclusion that more aircraft must be taken to sea. The first step was to set up a Grand Fleet Aircraft Committee under Rear Admiral Evan-Thomas to turn the Longhope directive into a reality. The new Commander-in-Chief of the Grand Fleet insisted that 'anti-Zeppelin machines' and ships large enough to carry them were an urgent priority.

The committee had its eye on a specific ship, the so-called 'large' light cruiser *Furious*, completing at the Elswick shipyard of Armstrong on the Tyne. Laid down in June 1915, she was a strange hybrid. Capable of 31 knots and armed with two single 45.7cm (18in) guns she had the thin armour of a light cruiser. After some arguing over the details it was agreed in March 1917 that HMS *Furious* would not receive her forward 45.7cm (18in) gun turret, and in its place would be built a hangar for four single-seater fighters and four two-seater reconnaissance aircraft. The 69.5m (228ft) flying-off platform ran from the hangar roof to the bow. The rest of the ship was unchanged, and she was completed by late June 1917.

The 14 officers and 70 ratings of the air group were commanded by Squadron Commander Ernest Dunning of the RNAS, and the initial complement was three Short seaplanes and five Sopwith Pups. Dunning

Above: The *Argus* was refitted not long before the outbreak of war in 1939 as a training carrier. Initially she could carry up to 20 seaplanes.

believed that it would be possible, given a strong wind, to improve on Eugene Ely's feat by landing on the *Furious* while she was underway.

A MAJOR MILESTONE

On 2 August he flew parallel to the ship into a 21-knot wind, while the ship was steaming at 10 knots. With the Pup close to stalling he side-slipped over the hangar roof and touched down in the centre of the runway, allowing a handling party to grab hold of special leather toggles on the trailing edge of the wings. This was the first time an aircraft had achieved a landing on a warship at sea. Dunning repeated his achievement five days later but damaged an elevator, and during a second attempt the Pup's engine stalled, and cart-wheeled over the starboard side. The pilot was drowned before he could be rescued.

The tragedy put an end to the experiments because landing on a moving ship was obviously a manoeuvre which could only be undertaken by the most skilled aviators. In September the momentous decision was taken to give *Furious* a much more extensive refit, including a landing deck to replace the aft gun turret, extending the full width of the ship. The major drawback of the ship was the retention of the large single funnel and bridgework on the centreline, where the turbulence of the hot gases would inevitably make landings very hazardous. Communication for

personnel and aircraft was provided by gangways connecting the two deck areas, so that aircraft could be moved forward after landing. Given the urgency, there was no question of re-siting the funnel and tripod mast, so when the ship re-emerged early in 1918 landings were still risky so she reverted to the expensive but safer method of launching her aircraft and trying to recover them after they 'ditched' alongside.

By June 1918 *Furious*' air group included 14 Sopwith Strutters and eight Sopwith 2F1 Camels, the latter specially modified to deal with the enemy's Zeppelins. They proved their worth in driving off an attack by German seaplanes, but this was a waste of the ship's potential. Permission was given to launch another attack on Tondern, the first by ship-launched aircraft against a land target. On 18 July HMS *Furious* and her escorting light cruisers and destroyers were in position off the Danish coast, only 129km (80 miles) from the target. When a sudden thunderstorm broke it was decided to stop the operation, but as it seemed to have been undetected by the Germans, it was merely postponed for 24 hours. This time there was no hitch and at 0313 hours the first Camel rolled down the launching ramp.

The objective was the headquarters of the German Naval Airship Division, comprising three huge Zeppelin sheds: the 239m (787ft) Toska, housing the airships *L.54* and *L.60*, and the 184m (603ft) Tobias and Toni, housing between them only a single captive balloon. The Camels achieved total surprise, giving the defenders only three minutes warning. The first three attackers seem to have carried out a gliding attack, diving low and pulling up to clear the shed. Their bombs went straight into the shed, igniting the millions of cubic feet of hydrogen contained in the envelopes of the two Zeppelins. Fortunately for the Germans the doors were open, so the huge fire did not destroy the shed, but the smoke from the funeral pyre of *L.54* and *L.60* spiralled up to 300m (1000ft) in the sky, according to eyewitnesses. Ten minutes later the second wave of three Camels hit Tobias, destroying the balloon but missing a load of nearby hydrogen cylinders.

THE SOPWITH CUCKOO

The six pilots now faced a long trip back to the carrier. Three, believing they were running out of fuel, landed in neutral Denmark. Two reached the *Furious* and 'ditched' safely, but the sixth was never seen again. At 0740 hours only four-and-a-half hours after launching the Camels, the ship increased speed to 20 knots and headed for home.

A new carrier, with none of the drawbacks of HMS *Furious*, had been in the pipeline since 1916. She was the Italian liner *Conte Rosso*, laid down in 1914 but suspended until the hull was bought in August 1916 for conversion to a carrier. As HMS *Argus* she was launched in December 1917, and was originally intended to have slit forward and after decks divided by a centreline funnel. The experience with HMS *Furious*, however, resulted in a flush-decked arrangement, and smoke diverted into ducts leading aft below deck-level. These changes took time, and she did not join the Fleet until September 1918.

After the Battle of Jutland the High Seas Fleet showed no appetite for action against the Grand Fleet, and British thoughts turned to ways of striking at the Germans in their heavily defended bases. The weapon was to be a new torpedo-armed aircraft, the Sopwith Cuckoo. This owed its existence to the foresight and energy of Commodore Murray Sueter, who had issued a secret memorandum to the Sopwith Company asking its designers to investigate the feasibility of a biplane armed with one or even two torpedoes, and having four hours endurance. Sueter also enquired

about the possibility of using catapults to launch the proposed torpedo-bomber, at a time when the Royal Navy had no catapult in service! The Cuckoo prototype flew in June 1917, a very advanced machine with folding wings, a wide undercarriage and a payload of a single 454kg (1000lb), 45.7cm (18in) torpedo. The name was chosen because of the cuckoo's habit of 'laying its eggs in other people's nests'.

HMS *Argus* was assigned a major role in the plan, being intended to launch a strike of 20 Cuckoos. Ninety were delivered by the armistice, earmarked for a major air-attack on the High Seas Fleet at Wilhelmshaven early in 1919. Production ceased almost immediately, but the Cuckoo was the ancestor of all the successful torpedo-bombers of World War II. Significantly, the Japanese bought six Cuckoo Mk. IIs in 1922.

In addition to the *Argus*, a second carrier was under construction. Ordered in April 1917, HMS *Hermes* was the first warship in the world designed to operate with conventional aircraft. On a displacement of 10,160 tonnes (10,000 tons) her aircraft complement was the same as the *Argus*, but unlike the *Argus*, she had an island superstructure and funnel set to starboard to provide a full-length flight deck. Although small, she had adequate speed for the day, 25 knots, and was a good seaboat. This ingenious ship was not laid down until January 1918, and was planned to enter service in 1921 (in fact she was delayed until 1925 by post-war economics).

To fill the gap the Admiralty decided in the autumn of 1917 to convert the hull of the incomplete Chilean battleship *Almirante Cochrane*. She had been suspended in 1914, but work was restarted, and she was formally purchased in February 1918 and named *Eagle*. Features already settled for the *Hermes* were incorporated, but as she was a much larger ship the hangar was considerably bigger. She was launched in June 1918, but was also delayed by the post-war slow-down in naval work.

Although the RNAS led the world in 1918 (it was absorbed into the new 'independent' Royal Air Force on 1 April 1918), other navies were also active in finding ways to get aircraft to sea. Since 1911 the US Navy had shown great interest in catapults. The first was tried by Lieutenant Theodore Ellyson at Glenn Curtiss' works at Hammondsport, New York in 1911, using a simple 'accelerator'. Captain Chambers, head of naval aviation, recognised the weakness of this contraption, and persevered with his design for compressed-air launching. This prototype catapult was

Above: HMS *Campania* after her second reconstruction with the forefunnel split to make room for a longer flying-off platform.

installed at the Santee Dock at Annapolis by June 1912. So sudden was its acceleration that it nearly killed Ellyson by stalling the engine of his Curtiss A-1 seaplane. Adjustments were made to the catapult, and on 12 November Ellyson made the first catapult take-off. In October 1915 a test-model was installed on the quarterdeck of the battleship USS *North Carolina*. The first launch from her deck was made on 5 November that year by Lieutenant-Commander Henry C. Mustin, flying a Curtiss AB-3. Early in 1917 similar catapults were installed in the armoured cruisers USS *Seattle* and USS *Huntington*. Although successful they were removed shortly after the USA's entry into the war, on the excuse that they would interfere with the ships' ability to convoy shipping.

Although the British favoured the take-off platform for launching spotters and fighters, the American experience was noted with interest. In 1916 the hopper barge *Slinger* was converted into a catapult trials ship, but the installation was very heavy, and for the moment the small platforms were regarded as adequate. Mention should also be made of an ingenious idea, a lighter fitted with a short take-off platform for a Sopwith Camel, towed behind a destroyer. The device worked, with Zeppelin *L.53* shot down by a Camel 2F1 in 1918. Other Harwich Force destroyers towed flying boats and balloons, the balloons proving useful as a navigation marker for returning aircraft. In April 1916 the Royal Navy submarine *E.22* was fitted

with an aft-facing ramp for launching a pair of Sopwith Schneider seaplanes. The object was to test the feasibility of taking seaplanes into the Heligoland Bight to attack Zeppelins, but the ramp hampered the submarine's performance. No further action was taken, because *E.22* was torpedoed by a U-boat on 25 April, the day after the abortive trials.

THE 'WOLF CUB'

The German Navy had already tried something similar. As early as January 1915 *U.12* was modified to allow her to carry a Friedrichshafen FF.29 seaplane on her forward casing. The idea was hatched between Kapitänleutnant Walter Forstmann, commanding the U-boat, and Oberleutnant zur See Friedrich von Arnauld de la Perrière, commander of the seaplane detachment at Zeebrugge on the Belgian coast. A successful flight was made over the coast of Kent, unobserved by the British, but rough seas prevented a rendezvous with *U.12*, and the seaplane returned to Zeebrugge. Further trials were stopped by the authorities, but the idea was resurrected late in the war for the last generation of U-boats. One other example of shipboard operations was the armed merchant cruiser SMS *Wolf*, which embarked a Friedrichshafen FF.33

Above: HMS *Engadine*, seen at Scapa Flow in 1918, missed her chance to report the course of the German High Seas Fleet due to faulty radio equipment.

seaplane in 1917. Nicknamed *Wolfchen* ('Wolf Cub'), the seaplane was intended to scout for targets for the *Wolf's* concealed guns, but was also armed with small hand-dropped bombs. Between March 1917 and February 1918 the 'Cub' proved invaluable, helping the *Wolf* to sink or capture six ships.

One last aspect of British naval aviation cannot be ignored. A large number of airships were built, mostly relatively small non-rigid 'blimps'. Although most flew from land bases, a few operated from carriers. As early as October 1914 a Naval Balloon Section was formed to support the Royal Naval Division in its ill-starred bid to defend Antwerp, but the port fell before the section could get to Belgium. Later that month Rear Admiral Hood asked for some balloons to be sent to the Belgian coast to direct the gunfire of his

scratch force of old battleships and gunboats bombarding the German right flank. The new division arrived at Dunkirk on 14 October, equipped with some spherical balloons dating from the Boer War. They proved of little use because of instability and a complex telephone link to the ships. By March 1915 copies of German kite balloons were being made, and plans were afoot for the Royal Navy's first balloon ship to spot for guns in the Dardanelles. The rugged Gallipoli peninsula was unsuitable for land-based balloons, so the decision was made to put them into ships.

THE BRITISH KITE BALLOON

The SS *Manica* was 15 years old, and took only 17 days to convert, with a long platform forward, a hydrogen compressor and winch and accommodation for the operators. As no British kite balloon yet existed a French type was borrowed. HMS *Manica* arrived at Mudros in April 1915, and was soon busy. The

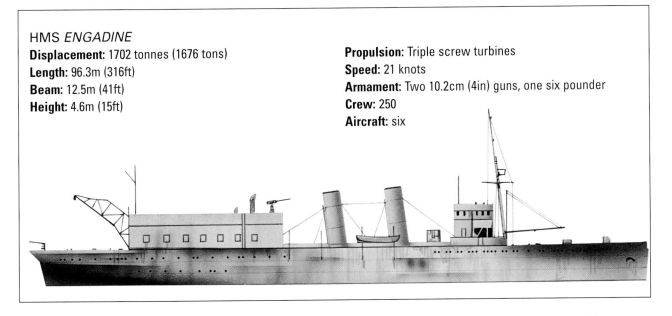

HMS *ENGADINE*
Displacement: 1702 tonnes (1676 tons)
Length: 96.3m (316ft)
Beam: 12.5m (41ft)
Height: 4.6m (15ft)

Propulsion: Triple screw turbines
Speed: 21 knots
Armament: Two 10.2cm (4in) guns, one six pounder
Crew: 250
Aircraft: six

balloon proved better for spotting than the *Ark Royal*'s seaplanes because of its superior telephone and radio links and longer endurance. In September 1915 she returned to England for a refit. The platform was replaced by a welldeck and she was equipped to operate a seaplane. From April 1916 to May 1917 she supported coastal operations in East Africa.

WW1 – A GLIMPSE OF THE FUTURE

Two more conversions followed, the *Hector* and *Menelaus*, the former joining the *Manica* in the Aegean and the latter being assigned to the Dover Patrol. In 1916 the *Menelaus* was relieved by the *City of Oxford*, which was converted from a dummy battleship. The *Manica* was relieved by HMS *Canning* at Mudros in October 1915. After service in the Salonika campaign the *Canning* returned to England in May 1916 carrying with her the wreckage of Zeppelin *L.85*, which had been brought down by the gunfire of British warships. Two additional small craft were also converted, the tug *Rescue* and the barge *Arctic*. HMS *Menelaus* was paid off in 1917 when the shortage of merchant ships became acute, but the *Canning* continued to operate with the Grand Fleet, and the *City of Oxford* was converted to a seaplane carrier for service in the Levant. Two additional minor conversions which have escaped the notice of most naval aviation historians are the armed merchant cruisers HMS *Kinfauns Castle* and HMS *Himalaya* (the latter with a temporary canvas hangar), which operated seaplanes early in 1915 against the German light cruiser *Königsberg* in the Rufiji River in East Africa.

Above: The *Engadine* was a converted cross-channel steamer attached to the Battle Cruiser Force. She later served with the Grand Fleet in the North Sea.

The success of the *Manica* and *Menelaus* in the Dardanelles encouraged the commander of the Grand Fleet Battlecruiser Force to press for reconnaissance balloons in the autumn of 1915. Trials with HMS *Engadine* in the Firth of Forth were followed by the establishment of another Naval Balloon Section at Rosyth under Rear Admiral Hood. When the *Campania* emerged from a major refit in April 1916 she too was equipped to operate a French 'M' type kite balloon. In May 1917 the light battlecruisers *Courageous* and *Glorious*, four light cruisers and three destroyers were ordered to be fitted with kite balloons and winches. In July 1917 more destroyers and a number of smaller escorts were fitted for balloons to spot submarines. The system was also taken up by the US Navy and the French Navy in 1917-18.

The impact of the aircraft on naval warfare in 1914-18 was profound, and although World War I operations were not as successful as many people claimed at the time, they were a good pointer towards future possibilities. In 1914 the aircraft was nowhere near as mature as the submarine, for example, but by the armistice aircraft design was sophisticated, and naval aircraft had been created for specific roles. Had the war gone on into 1919 even more might have been achieved. Even so, naval aviators had caught a vital glimpse of the future and seen that it was within their grasp.

CHAPTER THREE

Between the Wars

As the Royal Navy and US Navy continued to increase the size of their aircraft carrier fleets, and established standard carrier design guidelines, such as incorporating a starboard island superstructure, the Imperial Japanese Navy also embarked upon an ambitious carrier building programme. But not all was rosy, as worldwide economic depression hit defence budgets hard and slowed down shipbuilding programmes.

The end of the war in November 1918 inevitably brought an abrupt end to many promising developments in naval aviation. Yet however keenly the victors talked of beating their swords into ploughshares, within a year of the armistice latent tensions among the former allies became evident. For one thing, the United States had a new-found confidence, seeing itself as the moral leader of the world. Other nations might resent such pretension, but America's status as the world's major creditor could hardly be denied. Both the State Department and the Navy saw the need to challenge Britain's position as the premier naval power, using America's vast industrial base to outbuild the British as well as the Japanese if needed.

Left: An idealised view of the US Navy's *Lexington* class carriers. In fact, many US officers saw them as too expensive and too big to run.

The Royal Navy, supported by the resources of the Empire and its chain of bases around the world, was still the largest in the world. It also enjoyed the advantage of its large investment in naval aviation, putting it far ahead of any other navy. But the country was financially and spiritually debilitated after four years of bitter conflict. The Japanese, on the other hand, still basked in the glory of their decisive defeat of Imperial Russia in 1904-05, and had done extremely well out of the recent war, building ships and manufacturing war material for the European Allies.

Strongly influenced by the progress made in the Royal Navy, the Imperial Japanese Navy began design work on their own aircraft carrier in 1919. The *Hosho* was to be similar in size and speed to HMS *Hermes*, but instead of the island superstructure, she was to have three diminutive funnels set on the starboard side of the flight deck. These funnels were

27

hinged to allow them to be lowered to a horizontal position during flying operations. An island was planned, but after trials in 1923 it was removed. A relatively light armament allowed a complement of 26 aircraft, and as she was rushed to completion ahead of HMS *Hermes*, the *Hosho* qualified as the first purpose-built aircraft carrier in service.

FLEET REQUIREMENTS

The US Navy was also impressed by the *Hermes*. In 1917 naval constructor Stanley Goodall was sent to Washington on secondment to the Bureau of Construction & Repair (BuC&R), and with him he took not only the details of the *Hermes* but also all British wartime experience to date. In June 1918 the Director of Naval Aviation asked the General Board to put forward a requirement for a carrier, and Goodall was asked to comment on the proposals. In summarising British ideas, Goodall said, 'Such a type is essential for the British Navy … A fleet should … be attended by reconnaissance machines and fighting machines … An armament of four 10.2cm (4in) guns is insufficient, and a larger number of guns – preferably 6in (15.25cm) – should be carried, together with one or two anti-aircraft guns. Although such a ship should not by any means be regarded as a fighting ship, it should be sufficiently powerfully armoured to be able to brush aside light vessels of the enemy, so that its machines can be flown off in comparatively advanced positions. The speed proposed – namely 30 knots – is considered a minimum.'

In July 1920 the US Navy hoped to lay down four carriers over a period of three years, and a year later the construction of at least three was being talked of as a top priority. Lacking tactical experience, the US Navy had to rely heavily on war-gaming, and great attention was paid to the findings of the Naval War College. In 1922 a General Board Hearing was told that the previous year had been devoted to war-games with carriers taking part in various simulated engagements. All of them showed that aircraft could influence the outcome of, even if they could not dominate, a naval battle.

The planners were, however, moving too fast and Congress was determined to impose financial constraints. The United States was hardly impoverished after the economic activity in the recent war, but the mood of withdrawal from world affairs which set in after the Versailles Peace Conference in 1919 included a well-meaning commitment to reduce 'bloated armaments'. It was an article of faith among the intelligentsia on both sides of the Atlantic that the recent World War had been caused by the Anglo-German arms race. There was also a hidden agenda; US plans to build a huge fleet 'second-to-none' had alarmed both the Japanese and the British, who drew up plans for even larger capital ships. The United States had drawn up its grandiose plans in 1916, when Europe was preoccupied, but now it could look forward to an arms race of its own, committed to designs which were inferior to those of its potential enemies.

The General Board hoped to win approval for a large carrier equipped with 24 aircraft in Fiscal Year 1920 (FY '20). It originated in Goodall's proposal for a 22,353-tonne (22,000-ton), 244m (800ft) ship in August 1918. Two months later it had grown to 24,385 tonnes (24,000 tons) and speed had risen to 35 knots, with an armament of 10 15.25cm (6in) guns. In March 1919 the General Board decided to increase armament to four 20.3cm (8in) guns, six 15.25cm (6in), four torpedo-tubes and four 10.2cm (4in) anti-aircraft guns. Such a scale of armament demanded a bigger hull, and to expedite the process the General Board recommended the adaptation of a design for a 35,358-tonne (34,800-ton) battlecruiser, one of the proposals which led up to the 43,690-tonne (43,000-ton) *Lexington* class. The design featured two islands, one to port and the other to starboard, with the single 20.3cm (8in) guns forward and aft, and 15.25 (6in) guns on the broadside and aft. Normal displacement was calculated at just over 29,465 tonnes (29,000 tons), and to reach 35 knots 104,398kW (140,000hp) of power was specified.

THE 'COVERED WAGON'

Congress remained adamant, however, refusing to fund any carriers in either FY '20 or FY '21. The funds for conventional surface ships planned as far back as 1916 were drying up, and there could be no question of finding new funds for expensive novelties. All that could be afforded was the conversion of a big fleet collier, the *Jupiter* (AC-3), into an experimental carrier. The General Board was unhappy with the compromise, but took the view that any carrier was better than no carrier. She entered Norfolk Navy Yard in March 1920 for a two-year conversion, with her coal-handling derricks replaced by a 163m (534ft) wooden flight deck and her holds converted to hangars and fuel tanks. She was renamed *Langley* (*CV-1*) in honour of the 1911 pioneer. Nicknamed the 'Covered Wagon', she endeared herself to the aviators, and provided much-needed practical experience.

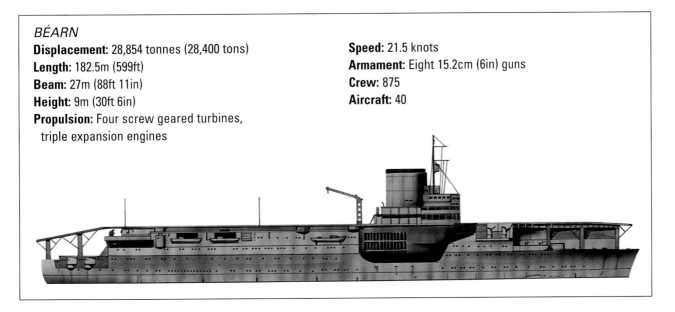

BÉARN
Displacement: 28,854 tonnes (28,400 tons)
Length: 182.5m (599ft)
Beam: 27m (88ft 11in)
Height: 9m (30ft 6in)
Propulsion: Four screw geared turbines,
  triple expansion engines

Speed: 21.5 knots
Armament: Eight 15.2cm (6in) guns
Crew: 875
Aircraft: 40

Above: The French Navy's carrier *Béarn* was converted from the hull of a battleship in the early 1920s. She proved too slow to be efficient.

The only other carrier to appear during this period was the Royal Navy's *Eagle*. She was, as we have already seen, a conversion from a Chilean battleship, launched in June 1918. Like the 1918-19 US Navy designs, she was designed with a double island, with a funnel and a tripod mast on each. There is intriguing mention of a 'bridge' between them, strong enough to carry four 10.2cm (4in) anti-aircraft guns and a navigating position, but practical experience with *Furious* and wind-tunnel tests ruled this out, and the now-familiar starboard island was substituted instead. Unlike the little island in the Japanese *Hosho*, the British ship had a long island, a heavy tripod foremast and two funnels. The configuration was recommended by Captain Nicholson of HMS *Furious* and Wing Captain Clark Hall of the RNAS. In spite of the Admiralty's intention to get the ship into service quickly she was not ready for sea trials until April 1920. Even so, she had only one funnel in place, two boilers, no lifts and an unfinished island, and could only be used for experimental flying. A new longitudinal arresting gear was transferred from the *Argus*, a series of wires extending 58m (190ft) – later increased to 98m (320ft) – to keep the aircraft correctly aligned rather than to slow them down. Landings were made by Camels, Cuckoos and Parnall Panthers, and these were sufficiently successful to allow the ship to return to dockyard hands for completion to the full design in September 1923.

Today the starboard island superstructure is taken for granted, but HMS *Eagle*'s captain regarded it as a serious handicap; the Naval Air Section said that it was a nuisance but helped the pilot by giving him a reference point for height and alignment. Wind-tunnel tests seemed to confirm these negative views, and proposals were made to shorten and widen the island in HMS *Hermes* and eliminate it entirely when HMS *Furious* was rebuilt. Much later research showed that pilots tend to turn to port if they make faulty landings, so a port island increases the number of serious landing accidents. Despite the aviators' insistence that all design features must be subordinated to the needs of pilots, the humble tasks of ship-handling and navigation made the island necessary, and also provided a convenient way of keeping funnel-gas and smoke clear of the deck. None of the schemes for dispersing smoke through deck-edge funnels or ducts were ever a great success, as they caused eddies and turbulence.

When HMS *Furious* docked at Devonport Dockyard in June 1922 she was given a 176m (576ft) flight deck, a double-storeyed hangar and retractable navigating bridges. The now somewhat dated concept of a launching ramp over the bow was retained, to allow fighters to take-off from the upper hangar with minimum delay. In the 1920s aircraft were still light enough to use such a method, but as the years went by it became less useful. In her new guise she was to prove effective, having the right combination of speed and aircraft capacity.

By the summer of 1922, less than two decades after the first ever powered flight, there were now three converted carriers in service (HMS *Argus*,

Above: When HMS *Furious* emerged from her third reconstruction in 1925, she was nicknamed by some as the 'covered wagon'.

HMS *Furious* and the USS *Langley*), a fourth nearly ready (HMS *Eagle*) and two purpose-built carriers nearing completion (HMS *Hermes* and HIJMS *Hosho*). It was no surprise that the Royal Navy led the field, but already the pernicious effects of a decision made four years earlier were becoming clear. Following two effective daylight raids on London by German bombers in 1917, the British Cabinet had been panicked into convening a committee to study the problems of air defence and aircraft procurement.

AIR POWER – A NEW CONCEPT

Under its chairman, the brilliant South African general, Jan Smuts, the committee spent two months preparing its conclusions. In its preamble it embraced a dazzling new concept of 'strategic air power', and looked to a future in which 'aerial operations, with their devastation of industrial and populace centres on a vast scale, may become the principal operations of war, to which the older forms of military and naval operations may become secondary and subordinate'. Another exponent of air power, the Italian theorist General Giulio Douhet, claimed that a future war might be won by bombers alone without the opposing armies and navies firing a single shot. Ironically, the first 'strategic' raids against targets inside Germany had been made by RNAS aircraft, but the new disciples totally ignored the paltry results of such raids.

The solution to the muddle and duplication in the supply of aircraft and training pilots between the RNAS and the RFC was to be the amalgamation of the two air services into a new Royal Air Force (RAF). Administratively, this was logical, and it was originally envisaged that the RAF would continue to divide its resources between land and air operations as the old RFC had done. But Smuts had turned his mind to much more contentious ideas. Once the present shortage of airframes and engines was overcome, he said, the surplus should be devoted to the formation of an 'independent' or 'strategic' bomber force to carry the war into Germany. The government accordingly formed a new Air Ministry in November 1917, and the formation of the RAF followed on 1 April 1918 – the world's first independent air force. Brigadier General Hugh Trenchard became the first Chief of the Air Staff and then Commander-in-Chief, and in addition took command of an Independent Bombing Force of British, French, Italian and American bombers, formed just before the armistice.

Being confined to administrative matters, the effects of these fundamental changes were hardly felt before the guns fell silent in November 1918. But the Air Staff was dominated by former RFC officers, and the naval viewpoint was overshadowed. Pilots were all to belong to the RAF, and naval pilots were encouraged to transfer to make up the numbers. This benefited the RAF, but the Navy was robbed of most of its keenest aviators; very few chose to remain loyal to the Navy when a brave new world beckoned. Thus, at a crucial stage in the evolution of naval tactics, the voice of naval aviation was seriously weakened. The Admiralty recognised the danger, and in 1924 the Fleet Air Arm was established as a branch of the RAF in its own right. In response, Trenchard and his supporters became obsessed with the need to maintain the independence of 'his' service. In their zeal they fastened on the strategic bombing role as the only worthwhile mission. Douhet's teachings were taken literally, despite the fact that the recent war was hardly proof of their validity. The debate became more and more unreal, with parrot-cries about the 'indivisibility of air power' and 'the bomber will always get through'. At every turn politicians and the press were bombarded with claims that any ship would be blown out of the water by 'precision' bombing, and spurious statistics to show that one battleship cost as much as 1000 bombers (it turned out to be only 37).

The claims of the bomber enthusiasts could be dismissed as boyish exuberance, but the practical effect was to siphon off the limited funds available for bomber production. The Fleet Air Arm had a very low priority, and as design and procurement of aircraft remained in RAF hands it would have been impossible for the most air-minded admirals to exert any influence over specifications. The results were soon evident; British naval aircraft, which were as good as they could be in 1918, dropped steadily behind those coming into service in the United States and Japan.

The US Navy had its own share of problems. After the armistice, US Army aviator Brigadier General William Mitchell began to press for an independent air force along the lines of the RAF. Like Trenchard,

'Billy' Mitchell was an army officer who had taken up flying quite late in his career, and like all converts he was evangelical. Unlike Trenchard, however, he chose to start his campaign in peacetime, when the overriding need for a quick solution was no longer a factor. In fact he found himself taking on not only the Navy but the Army as well, and the conflict was to be all the fiercer as a result.

BOMBERS VS. BATTLESHIPS

In November 1920 the Navy had initiated bombing tests against the old pre-dreadnought battleship *Indiana*, using bombs positioned carefully on board and allowing bombers to attack with dummy bombs purely for target-practice. Mitchell watched these tests and was delighted to see the *Indiana* sink. What he could not or would not admit was that the on-board detonations had achieved the sinking and that the bombers had dropped dummy bombs. Equally important was the fact that the battleship was old and small, and had no protection of any kind against bombs. He also ignored the Navy's insistence that scientific trials were the only means of learning any valuable lessons.

Ignoring this reasonable attitude, Mitchell continued to press for the formation of a separate 'Air Department'. As both sides dug in, the argument increasingly took the form of 'bombers vs. battleships', with nothing in between. As he intended, the

Below: Although relatively slow, HMS *Eagle* incorporated several advanced features, and performed well enough in World War II. She was sunk in 1942.

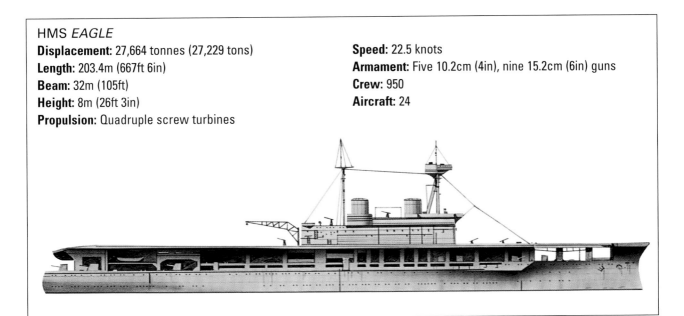

HMS *EAGLE*
Displacement: 27,664 tonnes (27,229 tons)
Length: 203.4m (667ft 6in)
Beam: 32m (105ft)
Height: 8m (26ft 3in)
Propulsion: Quadruple screw turbines

Speed: 22.5 knots
Armament: Five 10.2cm (4in), nine 15.2cm (6in) guns
Crew: 950
Aircraft: 24

Navy Department was put under strong pressure by the press and Congress to give the pilots a chance to prove their point. The Navy agreed to stage a series of tests in June-July 1921, using surrendered German warships as targets.

The tests had a strong element of farce about them. Despite the claims of the Army Air Service Department's bomber-enthusiasts, radios, compasses and even bomb-sights had to be borrowed from the Navy, while ships had to be stationed off the coast to help locate the targets. Furthermore, Army air crews had never flown as far as 90km (60 miles) from land. On 21 June the first test began with three Navy flying boats attacking a U-boat, each armed with three 82kg (180lb) bombs. The *U.117* sank 12 minutes after the first hit. Next it was the turn of a contemporary of the *Indiana*, the *Iowa*, also attacked by Navy bombers with dummy bombs. The Navy claimed that the Army bombers should not be allowed to bomb her as she was 'cheating' by manoeuvring under radio control. Given the crude navigation of the day, it is doubtful if the Army pilots could have found her, let alone hit her. The destroyer *G-102* and the light cruiser *Frankfurt* followed soon after, hit by heavy bombs.

The three ships sunk so far had been either very old or small, but the final test was to be against a modern battleship, the 23,166-tonne (22,800-ton) *Ostfriesland*. Built in 1911, she had fought at the Battle of Jutland, but was designed at a time when air attack was no threat. Nevertheless, the prestige of German battleships was high, and Mitchell's support-

Below: The *Furious* was the result of a planned fleet of fast, powerful carriers with shallow draught to operate in the Baltic against Germany's northern coast.

ers took care to spread the rumour that the *Ostfriesland* was 'unsinkable'. In fact she was in poor condition, and had needed repairs before she could cross the Atlantic in safety.

THE BATTLESHIP OF THE FUTURE

On 20 July Navy and Marine Corps pilots dropped 34 light bombs on the battleship, of which six hit. An inspection of the damage should have followed, but without warning six Army bombers arrived and dropped a number of 272kg (600lb) bombs, of which only two hit. This time the inspection was carried out as planned, and the *Ostfriesland* was found to have suffered no appreciable damage between decks. Next day eight Army MB-2 bombers each dropped two 454kg (1000lb) bombs and scored six hits, but the inspection team reported that the ship was still seaworthy. The bombers returned in the afternoon and dropped 908 kg (2000lb) bombs, the heaviest in the world. One bounced off, two missed and the fourth hit, but even after these hits the battleship took the rest of the day to sink, with no fire parties or damage control teams on board to cope with flooding.

The less than decisive result did not prevent Mitchell and his partisans from claiming a resounding success, the sinking of a battleship by air attack. It was, however, far from being 'the day the admirals wept', as the myth-makers pretended. Although three obsolete battleships were later sunk by Army bombers, the chance to test bombing against a modern battleship did not occur until November 1924. The unfinished super-dreadnought *Washington* was subjected to systematic bomb- and torpedo-attacks, as well as gunfire. The report tended to vindicate the Navy's view: 'The battleship of the future can be so

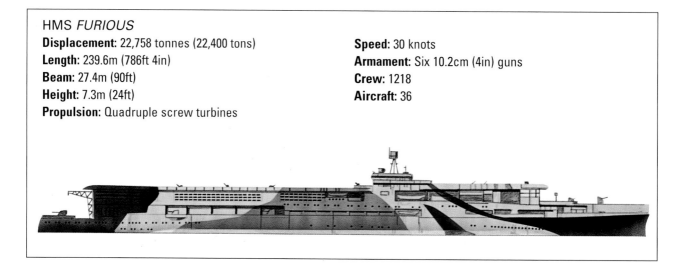

HMS *FURIOUS*
Displacement: 22,758 tonnes (22,400 tons)
Length: 239.6m (786ft 4in)
Beam: 27.4m (90ft)
Height: 7.3m (24ft)
Propulsion: Quadruple screw turbines

Speed: 30 knots
Armament: Six 10.2cm (4in) guns
Crew: 1218
Aircraft: 36

Above: Observer's eye-view of HMS *Furious,* showing the plume of steam on the flying-off deck to indicate she is steaming into wind.

designed as to distribution of her armour on decks and sides, and as to interior subdivision, that she will not be subjected to fatal damage from the air. It cannot be said, therefore, that air attack has made the battleship obsolete.' This verdict reflected accurately the current capabilities of bombers, and even 20 years later high-level bombing would continue to disappoint its supporters. In the long term the carrier-borne aircraft would prove themselves over the big guns.

Mitchell, it was said, asked for his court martial and got it, when in 1925 he accused the US Navy of 'almost treasonable incompetence' leading to the loss of the large rigid airship *Shenandoah* in a storm. He had done a great deal of good for land-based aviation, and in the long run he helped to assure the future of the big aircraft carrier, but he had also done a great deal of harm. He set the Navy and the Army Air Corps at each other's throats, and focused attention, not only in the United States but elsewhere as well, on high-level precision bombing. In World War II the RAF's faith in high-level bombing at sea proved totally misplaced, as it did for the Italian *Regia Aeronautica.* Only in those air forces which showed an interest in dive-bombing and torpedo-dropping did tactics begin to evolve along the right lines.

In November 1921 President Harding convened a naval disarmament conference in Washington to discuss ways of heading off a naval arms race between the United States, Japan and Great Britain. The main area of disagreement was the large number of battleships being built in Japan and the United States, and the delegates addressed themselves to the task of persuading the three major navies to cut back their surface fleets. The result was that Britain and the United States agreed to retain 15 capital ships (battleships and battlecruisers), Japan accepted a limit of nine and France and Italy were allowed five each. Largely as a sop to their wounded pride the navies were allocated tonnage totals for aircraft carriers: 137,166 tonnes (135,000 tons) each to the Royal Navy and the US Navy, 82,300 tonnes (81,000 tons) to Japan and 60,963 tonnes (60,000 tons) each to France and Italy. The extra tonnage allowed to the Americans and British was for conversion of cancelled or redundant hulls to avoid unemployment in shipyards, but it provided the excuse to build carriers at a time when funds for new construction would have been extremely difficult to justify.

The final draft of the Washington Naval Disarmament Treaty provided the first formal definition of an aircraft carrier: a warship displacing over 10,160 tonnes (10,000 tons) but not more than 27,433 tonnes (27,000 tons), designed for the specific and exclusive purpose of carrying, launching and landing

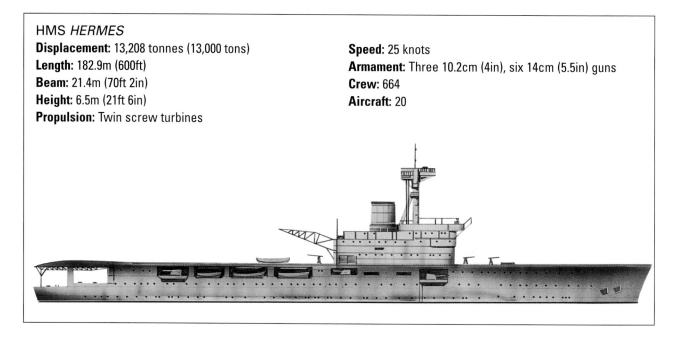

HMS *HERMES*
Displacement: 13,208 tonnes (13,000 tons)
Length: 182.9m (600ft)
Beam: 21.4m (70ft 2in)
Height: 6.5m (21ft 6in)
Propulsion: Twin screw turbines

Speed: 25 knots
Armament: Three 10.2cm (4in), six 14cm (5.5in) guns
Crew: 664
Aircraft: 20

aircraft. Guns were not to exceed 20.3cms (8-inches) in calibre, and not more than 10 were to be carried. As a special concession the Americans and Japanese were each permitted to convert two carriers of 33,530 tonnes (33,000 tons) to make use of existing hulls. These were the rules which governed carrier design for nearly 20 years, until World War II made them redundant.

THE 'LEX' AND 'SARA'

The US Navy's Bureau of Construction & Repair had been considering the conversion of a battlecruiser design since 1919. Since the six *Lexington* (CC.1-6) class battlecruisers were almost certain to be axed by the 1922 Treaty, the Chief of Preliminary Design on his own initiative ordered a detailed study to be made in July 1921. As a result, when the delegates reached their momentous decision early the following year, the BuC&R was well advanced in the preparation of the design. The ships selected for conversion were the *Lexington* (CC.1), building at Bethlehem's Quincy yard in Massachusetts, and the *Saratoga* (CC.3), building by the New York Shipbuilding company at Camden, New Jersey. They were the most advanced of the six, and would therefore need less money to complete the conversion. Even so, the estimated cost was $22.4 million, excluding the money already spent, and actual costs proved higher.

The designers' biggest problem was the arbitrary limit of 33,530 tonnes (33,000 tons), which had been chosen to satisfy the Japanese. The planned displacement for the new US Navy carriers had been initial-

Above: Although small, HMS *Hermes* introduced valuable features such as the starboard island superstructure. She was sunk by Japanese carrier aircraft off Ceylon in 1942.

set at 41,658 tonnes (41,000 tons), and had then been cut to 39,626 tonnes (39,000 tons) and finally settled at 36,578 tonnes (36,000 tons). It proved impossible to 'lose' another 3048 tonnes (3000 tons) and so the General Board decided on a piece of sleight of hand. The Treaty allowed all existing capital ships to be modernised to improve defence, with additions limited to 3048 tonnes (3000 tons). The Board argued, unconvincingly, that the '3000-ton clause' applied to the ships *before* they were converted to carriers, so the 36,578-tonne (36,000-ton) figure did not breach the Treaty. However, the US Navy still listed the standard displacement as 33,530 tonnes (33,000 tons), leaving open the option to add another 3048 tonnes (3000 tons) at a later date.

The 'Lex' and 'Sara' were commissioned at the end of 1927 as *CV.2* and *CV.3* respectively, but their size drew heavy fire from critics, who derided them as white elephants. Lobbyists demanded their replacement by a larger number of small carriers, or the proliferation of catapult-launched aircraft through the Fleet, even in destroyers. Time was to show that all these options were wrong. The size of the *Lexington* and *Saratoga* permitted a designed air group of 78 aircraft (in practice 80 or 90 could be operated), allowing the 'mix' of bombers, scout planes and fighters to be varied according to the requirements of the mission. A series of 'Fleet Problems' or war

Above: A bomb burst obscures the hull of the German battleship *Ostfriesland* during the controversial trials in June-July 1921.

games was held annually from 1928 onwards, with the two sisters often matched against each other to test theories of aircraft carrier tactics. In service only one major design-error ever appeared: the inclusion of four twin 20.3cm (8in) gun turrets. Mounted forward and aft of the island, these mountings and their magazines encroached on valuable hangar-space, the substantial muzzle-blast was a danger to any aircraft on deck, and they contributed only a theoretical defence against attack by hostile cruisers. But, when the original design was conceived, carrier aircraft offered no guarantee against surface attack, and these disadvantages did not become fully apparent for a number of years.

Everything about them was on a colossal scale. The turbo-electric machinery developed 134,226kW (180,000hp) and drove them at over 33 knots. With 6775 tonnes (6668 tons) of fuel they could steam nearly 32,000km (20,000 miles) at 15 knots. Above all, their appearance was majestic, with a massive funnel combining the uptakes of all 16 boilers and they retained much of the grace of the original battle-cruiser. When the city of Tacoma ran short of hydro-electric power during a drought in December 1929 the USS *Lexington* was sent from Bremerton Navy Yard to generate power for the city's 100,000 inhabitants. She lay in a specially dredged berth for a month, coupled to the shore by power-lines, supplying the unbelievable total of 4.25 million kilowatt-hours.

Carrier tactics developed rapidly. In Fleet Problem VIII in 1928 planes from the USS *Langley* raided Pearl Harbor, taking the garrison and the defending

fleet by surprise. Fleet Problem IX the following year saw both *Lexington* and *Saratoga* participating, but the results were somewhat confusing. The *Saratoga*'s aircraft claimed a successful attack on the Panama Canal, but she was claimed 'sunk' previously by a battleship force and was subsequently 'sunk' by the *Lexington*'s air group; Navy land-based bombers then 'sank' their own carrier, the *Lexington*, instead of the 'hostile' *Saratoga*. If these war games sound childish, we must remember that their most important dividend was to formulate and exercise procedures, rather than to win or lose. What was evolving was technique, on the flight deck, in the hangar, and on the flag bridge. Only by playing such exuberant games could the admirals and captains learn to handle carriers with the same dexterity and confidence enjoyed by their contemporaries in battleships.

Across the Pacific the Japanese were busy with their own plans. Under the Washington Treaty they were permitted to convert the hulls of two 41,861-tonne (41,200-ton) battlecruisers, the *Akagi* and *Amagi*. On 1 September 1923, however, the *Amagi*'s

newly-launched hull was badly damaged in the great Tokyo Earthquake, and the other signatories agreed to allow the slightly smaller hull of the battleship *Kaga* to be substituted.

AKAGI AND *AMAGI*

When they first appeared they struck the same bizarre note as other contemporary Japanese warships, with flying-off decks forward at three levels, one a part of the forward end of the flight deck, and two serving the hangars. They carried the heavy armament of 10 20.3cm (8in) guns each, but their most grotesque features were their funnels. In the *Akagi* the forward funnel curved downwards and the second stuck out horizontally, whereas the *Kaga*'s was carried right aft horizontally. Their aircraft capacity was slightly less than the American conversions, a penalty imposed by the heavier armament. They were only partially successful, and had to be rebuilt a decade later along more conventional lines. But they served the same purpose as the *Lexington* and *Saratoga*: developing the concept of fast carrier task forces working as a major component of the Fleet.

BRITISH LAG BEHIND

The other runners in the race lagged far behind. The British lacked large hulls suitable for conversion, having only two half-sisters of the *Furious*, the light batlecruisers *Courageous* and *Glorious*. They were, however, lightly armoured and fast, so never suffered from the weight penalties of converted capital ships. HMS *Furious* herself emerged from her major reconstruction in September 1925 with a full-length flush flight deck, no island and smoke-ducts running right aft, as in HMS *Argus*. When HMS *Courageous* rejoined the Fleet in 1928 she had an island superstructure, and her sister, *Glorious*, joined in 1930.

With three carriers forming an homogenous group the Royal Navy could evaluate the claims for a larger number of small carriers, as against giants like the American and Japanese ships. But for obvious reasons they could not carry the same number of aircraft. Between them the three new carriers could operate 108 aircraft, whereas the *Lexington* and *Saratoga* could operate 160-180 between them, and on at least one occasion packed in 240. The *Akagi* and *Kaga* could also outmatch the three British carriers, with 140 aircraft between them. Another problem for smaller carriers is the limited amount of fuel carried, both for themselves and for their aircraft. The *Lexingtons* each carried some 600,083 litres (132,000 gallons) of high-octane gasoline (avgas) in specially protected tanks deep in the hull, as well as lubricating oil, whereas HMS *Furious* carried only 109,106 litres (24,000 gallons) of avgas and 18,184 litres (4000 gallons) of lube oil, and HMS *Eagle* could only manage a miserable 36,368 litres (8000 gallons) in all. There could be no question of these ships operating in the Pacific, and even in the European theatre their operational flexibility was limited by lack of endurance.

The only other nation to get an aircraft carrier into service during this period was France. She too had battleship hulls suitable for conversion, the five *Normandie* class laid down in 1914 but suspended during the war. In 1920 plans were drawn up to convert the *Béarn*, and the Washington Treaty clinched the matter. In April 1922 the conversion was authorised. Anglo-French cooperation was limited, but in desperation the *Marine Nationale* turned to the Royal

Above: The US Navy promoted aviation between the wars, encouraging some of its brightest officers to become aviators.

Navy for technical assistance, acquiring details of HMS *Eagle*. As a result *Béarn* incorporated useful British features such as fire precautions in the hangar, but she was also too slow; at 21.5 knots there was rarely enough wind over deck to ensure trouble-free flying. Aircraft were becoming heavier, and the wind over the deck began to assume much greater importance for landing and take-off.

The French carrier had a starboard island, and a unique ventilating system for diluting her funnel gas with cold air to reduce turbulence over the deck. Another unique feature was pairs of giant, hinged doors over the three deck lift wells, forming part of the flight deck. In other navies' carriers the lift platform served as part of the deck when in the 'up' position. The upper hangar held 40 aircraft, and spares and workshops were located in the lower hangar. The French Navy operated her successfully from 1927 but lack of funds prevented the purchase of more advanced aircraft, and the *Aéronavale* was never a serious challenge, even to the British Fleet Air Arm.

SPARVIERO
Displacement: 30,480 tonnes (30,000 tons)
Length: 202.4m (664ft 2in)
Beam: 25.2m (82ft 10in)
Height: 9.2m (30ft 2in)

Propulsion: Quadruple screw, diesel engines
Speed: 18 knots (as liner)
Armament: Six 15.2cm (6in), four 10.2cm (4in) guns
Crew: unknown
Aircraft: unknown

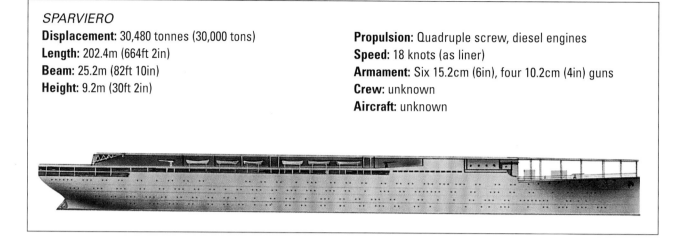

Despite their general enthusiasm for aviation the Italian Navy had no carriers. During the recent war the Navy had tried to form a naval air arm but the influence of General Douhet, recalled in 1917 to head the Central Aeronautical Bureau, was paramount. When in 1923 Mussolini took the Italian military down the path of Fascism, he followed the pattern of the RAF, unifying the Army and Navy air elements in a single 'independent' air service. *Il Duce* could not see the need for carriers, when in his opinion Italy was herself a big, unsinkable aircraft carrier. In 1925 he bullied his admirals into a policy statement denying the need for carriers, one they were to regret.

Several distinct features of design were by now well established. Flight decks were planked, usually

Above: The Italian Navy virtually ignored the aircraft carrier until World War II, when the *Sparviero* and others were converted from liners.

with teak, and the whole hangar structure was built on top of what naval architects call the 'strength deck'. Post-1918 this deck was usually armoured against bombs to protect the machinery and other vital parts from damage. Anti-aircraft and anti-ship guns were disposed around the edges of the deck, below the deck or grouped forward and aft of the island, wherever they had reasonable arcs of fire. Guns and carriers were never happy bedfellows; ammunition-supply was tricky and cross-deck firing damaged the deck and any aircraft nearby. In the early days the problem

USS *LEXINGTON*
Displacement: 35,438 tonnes (34,880 tons)
Length: 265.7m (871ft 9in)
Beam: 29.2m (96ft)
Height: 8.3m (27ft 6in)
Propulsion: Quadruple screws, turbines

Speed: 32.7 knots
Armament: Twelve 127mm (5in) guns
Crew: 2682
Aircraft: 91

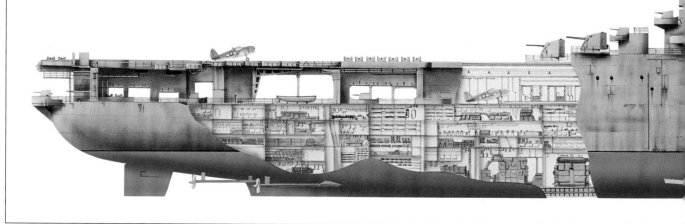

of ammunition-supply was largely ignored because no-one foresaw the weight of air attack which would be directed against carriers, but the positioning of guns was always a headache.

Ways of stopping aircraft once they had landed also called for new ideas, but the policies which emerged were erratic, to say the least. Following the unsuccessful schemes tried on HMS *Furious* in 1917, the British chose a system of longitudinal wires, but this was abandoned in 1926 because it tended to wrench the undercarriage too severely. A similar American system in the *Langley* and the *Lexingtons* was abandoned in 1929; it was felt that the big carriers' decks were so long that aircraft could brake in time. It was left to the French to revive an idea first tried in the *Furious* in 1917, a series of transverse wires, one of which had a good chance of snagging a hook fitted under the tail of the aircraft. The device was adopted by the Japanese and then by the British for HMS *Eagle* in 1933, and soon became standard. At the same time the crash barrier was reintroduced, a transverse screen capable of stopping any aircraft whose tailhook failed to engage a wire. This simple innovation enabled taking-off and landing to proceed simultaneously, and did much to speed up flight deck operations.

Below: The *Essex* class carrier *Lexington* (CV.16) was renamed after the old 'Lex' was sunk in the Coral Sea Battle in 1942.

The most frightening danger was fire. With thousands of gallons of avgas stored within the ship, giving off explosive vapours if allowed to leak, the smallest spark could destroy the ship. In the *Lexington* class fuel was stored in two single and six double tanks with a total capacity of 617 cubic metres (21,790 cubic feet), and fuelling points were provided in the hangar and on the flight deck. The British took even more trouble, and HMS *Eagle* introduced a new scheme, with avgas stored in bulk tanks, clear of the ship's hull and surrounded by air-spaces.

FIRE – THE GREAT DANGER

As part of their fire precautions British designers developed the concept of the 'closed hangar', in which the ventilation of the hangar was separated from the system provided for the rest of the ship. This enabled the hangar to be cleared of avgas vapours without the risk of dispersing them throughout the ship. The integrity of the closed hangar was preserved by air-locks in the bays, through which personnel entered the hangar. The Fleet Air Arm's use of higher-octane fuel caused problems because it was more corrosive and necessitated the use of special steel for avgas tanks. The disadvantage of the closed hangar was its encroachment on hangar space, further reducing the complements of aircraft in Royal Navy carriers. When the US Navy came to consider successors to the *Lexington* class there was considerable support for 'open hangars' extending out to the ship's side.

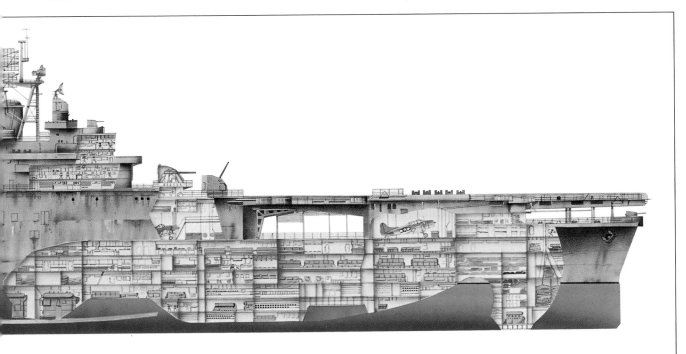

Above: Three first-generation US Navy carriers: (left to right) the *Lexington, Saratoga* and *Langley* in Puget Sound Navy yard.

The problem of ventilating the hangar would be dealt with by providing roller shutters, which could be opened to allow a through draught to assist the ship's ventilation system. It should be noted, however, that the heart of the Royal Navy system was the provision of a separate ventilation system, and attention to the fuel-lines which transferred avgas from the tanks to the hangar and flight deck.

To control the spread of fire in the hangar steel fire-curtains were provided, in the hope that a major fire could be contained. In 1929 the Fleet Air Arm introduced seawater-sprays in HMS *Eagle's* hangar, and this proved to be much more effective in containing fires. The saltwater corroded the light alloy airframes and their fabric wing-coverings, but that penalty was accepted, and this innovation marked the beginning of much improved damage control. The *Eagle* also introduced flight deck fire precautions in 1933, when she received four sets of foam-generators capable of covering the whole deck with a carpet of foam.

Despite their great length the *Lexington* class were fitted with a huge flywheel-driven catapult, 47m (155ft) long. Set in the forward part of the flight deck, flush with the upper surface, it could launch a 5.08-tonne (5-ton) aircraft at the modest speed of 48 knots.

Like *Langley's* catapults, it was seldom used, the aircraft of the day being light enough to take-off unaided. The two catapults were removed from the *Langley* in 1928, and the big carriers lost theirs in 1934.

DEPRESSION HITS DEFENCE

The US Navy planners were well aware of the need to exploit the knowledge gained from its three carriers, and in 1927 the General Board drew up plans for a five-year programme. As a reaction to the size of the *Lexington* class it was proposed to reduce displacement to 14,021 tonnes (13,800 tons), and to lay down one a year from 1929 to 1933. But the public mood was hostile to defence expenditure, and when the Depression came, defence spending was the first to be cut. Eventually the need to provide employment in the shipyards overcame isolationism, and funds for one new carrier were grudgingly voted. The ship was laid down in September 1931 and designated *CV.4*, later to be named the *Ranger*. She was not an unqualified success. The reduced displacement resulted in a lower speed of 29 knots, although her 75-strong air group was impressive. The original flush deck design had been dropped, and she was given a small island and two pairs of three folding funnels further aft, like the Japanese *Hosho*. These were interconnected to allow funnel-smoke to be directed to the lee side so as to cause minimum disruption of flying operations. But, all in all, the US Navy was lucky that the General Board was not allowed to order four more *Ranger* type. Before she was completed, carrier doctrine had changed, and the future minimum displacement was fixed at 20,321 tonnes (20,000 tons).

The Japanese tried to go one better, and took advantage of the clause in the Washington Treaty which exempted carriers below 10,160 tonnes (10,000 tons). In November 1929 they laid down the *Ryujo*, designed to displace only 8128 tonnes (8000 tons) and carry 48 aircraft. Despite the restricted dimensions the designers crammed in a two-storeyed hangar and a dozen 12.7cm (5in) guns, and gave her the same speed as the *Ranger*. But, whereas the American carrier fell short of the Navy's hopes, the *Ryujo* came close to being a disaster. Too much had been attempted on the displacement, and she was nowhere near her intended standard displacement of

8128 tonnes (8000 tons). Shortly after she was commissioned, the Imperial Japanese Navy suffered two disasters at sea, in which a new torpedo boat capsized and the Combined Fleet suffered severe damage in a typhoon. The new carrier's stability came under close scrutiny, and as a result four guns were removed, with as much topweight as possible. Unfortunately it was also necessary to raise the forecastle to improve seakeeping, and this cancelled out the weight-reductions. Finally, some 2540 tonnes (2500 tons) of ballast had to be added, a load which reduced speed considerably.

When it is considered that much of this activity took place during a world recession, and within the restrictions of the Washington Treaty, the progress in carrier design between 1922 and 1933 is remarkable. The second-generation carriers had their faults, but in one way or another they tested theory and put it into practice. All survived to serve in World War II, some with great distinction, and without them the next generation could not have been so effective. The day of the carrier was fast arriving.

Above: The new carrier USS *Enterprise* (CV.6) after completion in 1938. The design developed into the magnificent *Essex* class.

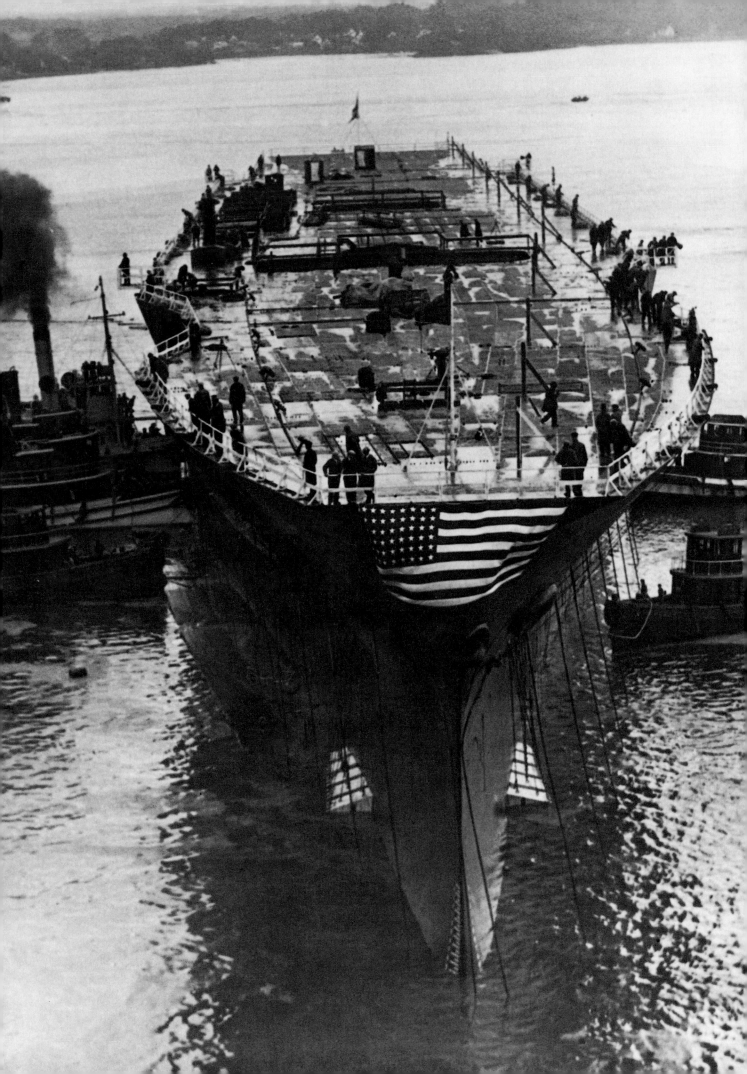

CHAPTER FOUR

The Third Generation

The Third Generation of aircraft carriers, which were built in the interwar years, took carrier design a step further. The new ships had large flight decks and incorporated many new features. Range was also a prime consideration, especially for the Americans, who came to realise that any future conflict they would be engaged in would be against the Japanese in the vast expanses of the Pacific Ocean.

In the United States shipbuilding was one of the major industries to receive government support during the long haul out of the Depression, and when in 1932 the Navy proposed the construction of two large carriers approval was given without any serious opposition. They would form part of the 1934 building programme but, as part of Roosevelt's 'New Deal' for America, would be funded by the Public Works Administration.

Left: The launch of the *Lexington* on 3 October 1925. She and her sister *Saratoga* (*CV.3*) were commissioned at the end of 1927.

The Bureau of Aeronautics was particularly anxious to avoid the mistakes made with the *Ranger*, and stipulated a minimum displacement of 20,321 tonnes (20,000 tons), a speed of 32.5 knots, increased protection against bombs and torpedoes, and above all, improved aircraft facilities. This last stipulation covered such matters as having a hangar deck dedicated entirely to aircraft stowage, more and faster lifts, better bomb-handling and even the possibility of two flying-off decks.

Not all the recommendations were incorporated into the design of the *Yorktown* (CV.5) and *Enterprise* (CV.6), but they were still a remarkable improvement

USS *ENTERPRISE*
Displacement: 25,908 tonnes (25,500 tons)
Length: 246.7m (809ft 6in)
Beam: 26.2m (86ft)
Height: 7.9m (26ft)
Propulsion: Quadruple screw turbines
Speed: 37.5 knots
Armament: Eight 12.7cm (5in) guns
Crew: 2175
Aircraft: 96

over previous carriers. They reverted to the starboard island configuration, carried 80 aircraft, had three centreline lifts and could steam at 33 knots. There was provision for three catapults, two flush-mounted on the flight deck and one athwartships in the hangar. In theory, the third catapult would allow more aircraft to be launched, but in practice it hampered movement in the hangar and was never used in wartime. An open hangar was retained, with the flight covered in 15.25cm (6in) teak planking laid athwartships. To assist in securing aircraft metal, tie-down strips were provided at 1.2m (4ft) intervals, running the full width of the deck. It was still believed that aircraft could be landed at either end of the flight deck, and two sets of arrester wires were provided. Like the hangar catapult, this feature proved impractical, and was soon dropped.

NEW JAPANESE DESIGNS

The Japanese had reached much the same conclusions as the Americans, and when they laid down the *Soryu* in November 1934 she displaced a nominal 19,101 tonnes (18,800 tons), carried 53 aircraft and, at 34 knots, was slightly faster than the *Yorktown* class. The London Naval Treaty of 1930 had agreed to extend the restrictions of the Washington Treaty, but the

Imperial Japanese Navy worked on the theory that if their next carrier was completed *after* the expiry of the treaty in 1936 it need not conform to the tonnage limit. As Japan had no intention of signing any more treaties, the sister of the *Soryu*, to be named *Hiryu*, could incorporate a number of improvements without the designers being inhibited by tonnage limits.

The disastrous experience of the Combined Fleet in the September 1935 typhoon also had a bearing on the *Hiryu*'s design, but her most unusual feature was recommended by the Navy's Aeronautical Bureau. Observing that the ideal position for a carrier's island superstructure was as close to the midpoint of the hull as possible, the Bureau recommended that *Hiryu*'s island should be close to midships. However, the designers also recommended that the funnels should be similarly positioned. To get around this, someone had the brilliant idea of putting the island on the port side. Human nature being what it is, a second reason was conjured up to justify the decision. Why not run the two near-sisters in line abreast when together, so that aircraft landing on the left-hand ship (*Soryu*) could fly in a left-handed semi-circle when picking up their formation or returning to land on the carrier? The other carrier would fly off and recover aircraft in the conventional manner, so the two formations

Above: The layout of the USS *Enterprise*, showing how the flight deck was built on the hull, rather than integral with it.

would be kept separate. Yet, as early British experiments in HMS *Argus* showed, pilots tend to veer to port if anything goes wrong during a landing, and the *Hiryu*'s pilots suffered roughly twice as many landing accidents as her sister.

The idea was taken a step further when the *Akagi* and *Kaga* were taken in hand for modernisation. They lost their unique triple flying-off decks and were rebuilt along more conventional lines in the late 1930s, with *Akagi* being given a port-side island. The idea was that she and her half-sister would be able to operate in a box formation with the *Hiryu* and *Soryu*. The modernisation was completed before the *Hiryu* was delivered, so the inherent flaws of the scheme were not yet apparent. Landing trials showed that the system would be unworkable, but by then it was too late to do anything about it.

The next pair of Japanese carriers were spared these tribulations. Ordered under the 1937 Fleet Replenishment Programme, the *Shokaku* and *Zuikaku* were not subject to treaty restrictions. On a standard displacement of 26,087 tonnes (25,675 tons) they operated 72 aircraft and could make 34 knots. No catapults were fitted as the light Japanese carrier aircraft could take-off using wind over deck, but eleven arrester wires were provided, three forward of the

crash barrier and eight aft. Two hangars were provided, served by three lifts (one on the centreline and two staggered to port and starboard). In the light of experience with the *Hiryu*, a small starboard island was provided; a scheme to have funnels on both sides was dropped, and instead smoke was exhausted through two starboard curved uptakes.

In many respects the *Shokaku* and *Zuikaku* were the best Japanese carriers yet and formed the basis of several later designs. There was no lack of freeboard, as with the *Ryujo*, and so they were dry forward. They were unusual in having a large Type 0 hydrophone under the bow, enabling them to detect the presence of submarines. Defensive armament was heavy: eight pairs of a new Type 89 twin 12.7cm (5in) anti-aircraft gun mounting, and a dozen triple 25mm (1in) light automatic weapons for close-range defence.

The Japanese Navy had evolved a different system of flight deck operations to the Americans and British. An Air Operations Officer and two junior officers were stationed on the bridge. On the flight deck was another officer responsible for the movements of aircraft such as taxiing. The take-off procedure was simple: the Air Operations Officer or his assistant held up a white flag, the signal for pilots to take-off at 20-second intervals. No further instructions were needed, and when the Air Operations Officer wished to end flying the flag was lowered. When the aircraft had to be recovered they flew downwind, about 350-550m (400-600 yards) from the carrier, and when the Flight Deck Officer or *Seibiin* was ready to let them land a flashing lamp signal was used. The pilot nearest the island then turned to arrive at a point about 730m (800 yards) astern of the carrier, at a height of about 180m (600 feet). There was no system of signals from the flight deck to help the pilot judge his approach, and so he relied on his own judgement. To help him he had a steam jet at the forward end of the flight deck, indicating the direction of the wind across the deck, and rows of lights down the centre of the deck and at the edges to indicate his height.

THE USA WELL AHEAD

Both the Americans and British had adopted the idea of a Landing Signals Officer (LSO), or Deck Landing Control Officer, more usually known as the 'batsman'. This was an experienced officer who held two 'paddles' shaped like table tennis bats and signalled to the pilot to correct his altitude, alignment and attitude as he approached the arrester wires with the 'sting' hook extended. If the aircraft was not likely to make a touchdown the batsman could give the pilot a 'wave-off' in time, allowing him to swing clear and make another circuit. This procedure reduced the risks considerably, although there was always the possibility that the tailhook would not properly engage, in which case the aircraft would plunge into the barrier.

The US Navy now took what might appear to be a retrograde step. Despite the recommendation of the Bureau of Aeronautics, the General Board sanctioned the building of a 15,377-tonne (14,500-ton) carrier, similar in size to the *Ranger*. The reason was that the Navy had used up most of its tonnage allowance under the London Naval Treaty, and the 15,377-tonne carrier would bring the total to 137,165 tonnes (135,000 tons), the maximum allowed. The new ship, designated CV.7, would, however, avoid the worst features of the *Ranger*, and was virtually a diminutive of the *Yorktown* design, sacrificing speed to retain the largest air group possible. Designed to have three centreline lifts, the forward one was replaced by a new type of T-shaped deck-edge lift on the port side opposite the island. The 'T' was just large enough to accommodate a single aircraft, with its undercarriage just below the crossbar and its tailwheel at the bottom end of the upright. When not in use it folded vertically, and its purpose was to speed up the transfer of aircraft from the hangar to the flight deck. As in the *Yorktown* class an athwartships catapult was provided. Although these innovations were not all successful, they proved that the US Navy had grasped the basic premiss that carrier aircraft are only effective when they become airborne. More than anything else this put the US Navy well ahead of other navies in its approach to carrier design.

The contract for the construction of CV.7 was awarded to the Bethlehem Steel Company in 1935 and she was launched in April 1939 as the USS *Wasp*. Events in Europe showed that the United States could

Below: The Japanese *Akagi* as built, with her unusual triple flying-off decks forward. *Akagi* led the attack on Pearl Harbor in 1941.

AKAGI
Displacement: 29,580 tonnes (29,114 tons)
Length: 248m (816ft 11in)
Beam: 30.5m (100ft)
Height: 8.1m (26ft 7in)
Propulsion: Four shaft turbines

Speed: 32.5 knots
Armament: Ten 20.3cm (8in), 12 11.9cm (4.7in) guns
Crew: 2000
Aircraft: 91

not avoid rearmament indefinitely, and the ship was commissioned a year later. As the peacetime complement of carriers was now complete the *Langley* was downgraded to a seaplane carrier, with nearly half her flight deck removed. The veteran had served the Navy well but was far too slow to work with the Fleet.

A SORRY STATE OF AFFAIRS

The British were also reluctantly coming to terms with the fact that 'collective security' and the League of Nations had not prevented the rise of Nazi Germany, and their own rearmament programme was launched in 1936. There were serious deficiencies, particularly in naval aviation. The Fleet Air Arm had not prospered under Air Ministry management, and was now in a perilous state. The RAF controlled aircraft procurement, and would not sanction the introduction of dive-bombers because it believed totally in high-level bombing, and the Navy was not encouraged to attempt to match the performance of land-based aircraft. Furthermore, the 'defection' of so many air-minded officers from the Navy to the RAF in 1918 was now making itself felt, and the Admiralty was dominated by senior officers who thought air power must be subordinated to the needs of the battle fleet.

Above: When the *Akagi* and her half-sister *Kaga* were rebuilt in the late 1930s, the forward end was rebuilt on more conventional lines.

RAF historians have blamed the Fleet Air Arm for some of its problems, caused by its insistence that all carrier aircraft must carry an observer, and must be rugged to withstand the shock of deck-landings. But these problems were confronted by the US Navy, and the blame must lie partly with the RAF and partly with the under-performance of the British aircraft manufacturers. It is hard to believe that an industry capable of producing the Hurricane and Spitfire could not produce something comparable for the Navy.

Nothing better illustrates the sorry state of affairs than the saga of the Fairey Swordfish. In 1933 the Fairey Aviation Company produced a design for a biplane Torpedo-Spotter Reconnaissance aircraft designated TSR.1, to compete against its own S.9/30, designed to an Air Ministry specification. It had a maximum speed of 220km/h (138mph) with a 45.7cm (18in) torpedo, and its defensive armament comprised a 7.7mm (.303in) machine gun fired by the observer, and a second machine gun firing through the propeller boss. In comparison, a year earlier the US Navy had ordered a prototype from Curtiss, designated the

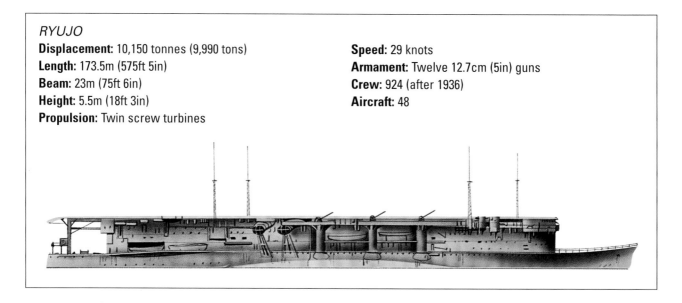

RYUJO
Displacement: 10,150 tonnes (9,990 tons)
Length: 173.5m (575ft 5in)
Beam: 23m (75ft 6in)
Height: 5.5m (18ft 3in)
Propulsion: Twin screw turbines

Speed: 29 knots
Armament: Twelve 12.7cm (5in) guns
Crew: 924 (after 1936)
Aircraft: 48

XF12C-1, a two-seat fighter intended to be capable of dive-bombing as well. Its parasol wing was not strong enough for dive-bombing, and like the prototype Swordfish it crashed during testing. In 1935 it reappeared as a biplane, the XSBC-2, capable of scouting and bombing, and having a speed of 352km/h (220mph). Even the Douglas T2D twin-engined torpedo-bomber which flew experimentally off the USS *Langley* in 1927 had a top speed nearly as high as the Swordfish six years later. More to the point, the Japanese Aichi D1A biplane dive-bomber, also ordered in 1933, had a top speed of 272km/h (174mph). The task of designing a suitable carrier-borne fighter was not simple. The design had to include several characteristics in order to achieve a balance: sufficient speed to intercept hostile aircraft, sufficient range to escort dive- and torpedo-bombers, ruggedness and restricted dimensions. This meant that naval fighters tended to be heavier than their land counterparts, but they were also more flexible. Happily, technology gradually came to the aid of the designer and folding wings and landing flaps to improve low-speed handling were among some of the advances made.

THE *ARK ROYAL*

It was against this confused background of good ideas but poor performance that the Royal Navy returned to the carrier business. The first fruit, HMS *Ark Royal*, was not only a remarkable technical achievement but was also destined to become one of the most famous aircraft carriers of World War II. When in 1930 the British and Americans locked the shackles of the Washington Treaty firmly to their wrists for another

Above: With the *Ryujo* the Japanese naval designers wanted to create a powerful carrier on a small displacement, but failed.

five years, the Admiralty laid down a new policy for the Fleet Air Arm. Five large carriers, each with a capacity of 72 aircraft, were to be built to replace the *Argus*, *Furious*, *Eagle*, *Courageous* and *Glorious* over a period of 25 years. As part of a general British initiative to limit expenditure on armaments, the Admiralty campaigned for a limit of 22,353 tonnes (22,000 tons), rather than the new 27,433-tonne (27,000-ton) limit agreed in the London Naval Treaty. When the first of the new British carrier programme was authorised in 1934 she conformed to the lower displacement.

Inevitably, the need for the new carrier was bitterly disputed by the RAF, which feared that any improvement in the Fleet Air Arm's position would be achieved by a reduction of its own allocation. A broader-minded approach might have been to make common cause with the Navy against the politicians, to put the case for both services. Unfortunately the RAF always suffered from the inferiority complex of being the 'junior service', and devoted an inordinate amount of its time and energy to nurturing the myth of the 'indivisibility of air power'. Any doctrine of naval air power clashed violently with the theories of strategic bombing held by them at the time, but in spite of many lurid claims about the ability of aircraft to sink ships, the RAF did nothing to develop dive-bombing, nothing about torpedo-bombing and precious little about sinking submarines.

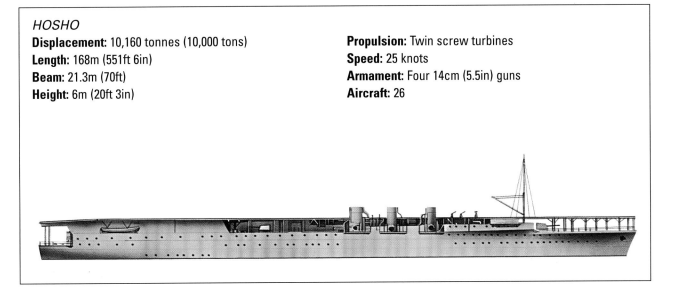

HOSHO
Displacement: 10,160 tonnes (10,000 tons)
Length: 168m (551ft 6in)
Beam: 21.3m (70ft)
Height: 6m (20ft 3in)

Propulsion: Twin screw turbines
Speed: 25 knots
Armament: Four 14cm (5.5in) guns
Aircraft: 26

The British financial position did not allow the new carrier to be ordered until 1935. The name *Mercury* had been considered, but it was later decided that she should bear the name of the first carrier. The old seaplane carrier was renamed *Pegasus* just before the new *Ark Royal* was launched in April 1937. Uppermost in the minds of the design team was the need to provide the maximum area of flight deck on the limited displacement, so the ship was given a remarkable degree of overhang forward and aft, 24.3m (80ft) in all. The machinery was designed for the abrupt accelerations and decelerations made by carriers to adjust the speed of wind over deck; in effect *Ark Royal*'s machinery had the power-output of a battleship but the characteristics of a destroyer. Tank testing showed that a shorter and beamier hull would be appropriate, and so instead of the 9 or 10:1 ratio favoured in the *Yorktown* and *Hiryu* designs, the *Ark Royal* had a ratio of 7.6:1, giving a good turn of speed without sacrificing stability or seakeeping. The system of stowing avgas remained unchanged from previous Royal Navy carriers, with 386 tonnes (380 tons) in cylindrical tanks separated from the hull to prevent rupture from the whipping of the hull in an explosion. However, for the first time the saltwater displacement system was replaced by compressed air, avoiding the risk of contaminating the fuel.

As with the American and Japanese carriers, there flight deck and hangars were left unprotected, but the magazines, avgas tanks and machinery were protected by a 8.9cm (3.5in) armoured deck at the level of the lower hangar deck. Protection against shellfire and torpedoes was provided by 11.4cm (4.5in) side armour, a shallow anti-torpedo 'bulge' and

Above: The Japanese *Hosho* was a contemporary of HMS *Hermes*, but she had triple folding funnels to leave the flight deck clear.

a 3.8cm (1.5in) internal anti-torpedo bulkhead. The ship was calculated to be safe against 15.25cm (6in) shellfire from cruisers at ranges of 6400m (7000 yards) or more, 227kg (500lb) bombs dropped below 2137m (7000ft) and a hit from a 340kg (750lb) torpedo warhead.

Two hangars were provided, with good overhead clearance and the usual excellent fire-precautions, including steel-slat fire curtains, saltwater sprays and air-locks to prevent avgas vapour from spreading outside the hangars. But all this carried a penalty, and by the time the design was finalised aircraft complement had gone down from 72 to 60. Unlike earlier American and British carriers, the *Ark Royal*'s flight deck was steel, with a 'round-down' aft and a similar slope at the forward end. Ever since the wind-tunnel tests on models of the *Furious* and *Eagle* at the end of World War I the British had paid attention to aerodynamic factors, and in the *Ark Royal* even the island was aerofoil-shaped to reduce turbulence. This was very necessary to protect the fragile aircraft available for carrier work, whereas US Navy aircraft were so robust that little or no attention was paid to the shaping of carrier islands. In one respect the 'Ark' resembled the *Lexington* and *Saratoga*, with the flight deck forming the 'strength' deck or upper girder of the hull. This was made possible by avoiding the big openings in the side which were essential to the open hangar concept, but it led to the provision of comparatively small lifts because it was undesirable to pierce the

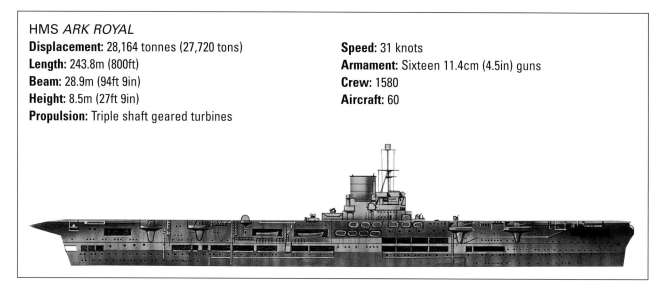

HMS *ARK ROYAL*
Displacement: 28,164 tonnes (27,720 tons)
Length: 243.8m (800ft)
Beam: 28.9m (94ft 9in)
Height: 8.5m (27ft 9in)
Propulsion: Triple shaft geared turbines
Speed: 31 knots
Armament: Sixteen 11.4cm (4.5in) guns
Crew: 1580
Aircraft: 60

main girder with large openings. Two lifts, forward and aft and set to starboard, were only 6.7m (22ft) wide, and the third, opposite the island to port, was 7.62m (25ft) wide. The 13.72m (45ft) length of these lifts allowed aircraft to be moved around the hangar easily when the lifts were in use, but British ingenuity overreached itself. Each lift had an upper and a lower platform, to assist in moving aircraft from the workshops in the lower hangar to the upper one, but it proved very slow and cumbersome when a defective aircraft had to be struck down from the flight deck to the lower hangar. The narrow lifts also meant that aircraft wings had to be folded before they could be moved up or down. The ship was given two hydro-pneumatic catapults at the forward end of the flight deck, but they differed from those in the *Yorktown* class in being 'accelerators' rather than true catapults. Whereas American catapults launched aircraft in the tail-down position, the *Ark Royal*'s required the aircraft to be raised on a trolley and then pushed forward on its own wheel at a speed approaching 66 knots. Eight arrester wires were provided, and a safety barrier, the first in a British carrier. The Fleet Air Arm had first tried a night landing on HMS *Furious in* 1926, and *Ark Royal* was provided with a comprehensive system, including deck-edge lighting and indicators of angle of descent and depth-perception. A further refinement was a series of recognition lights along the ship's sides to enable returning pilots to identify their own carrier, but this proved quite usless.

The amount of effort put into the design of HMS *Ark Royal* reflected a profound change in Royal Navy thinking. Growing disillusionment with RAF control had created a resurgence of 'air-mindedness' and

Above: The launch of the *Ark Royal* at Cammell Laird's shipyard in Birkenhead in 1937 coincided with the return of the Fleet Air Arm to naval control.

a new generation of admirals led a prolonged fight to win back control of naval aviation. Paradoxically, it was the RAF's obsession with strategic bombing which enabled the Navy to win the argument; naval aviation was becoming a tiresome distraction from the exciting task of building up a bomber force. In the summer of 1937 the government announced that responsibility for naval aviation was to be handed to the Navy over a period of two years, but the RAF was allowed to take back a large number of pilots and maintainers, creating major problems for the Navy.

The worsening situation in Europe meant that the original leisurely programme of laying down a carrier every five years had to be discarded. Only two years after the authorisation for the *Ark Royal* the 1936 Naval Estimates contained provision for two 23,369-tonne (23,000-ton) carriers. But instead of repeating the design, the Controller, Rear Admiral Reginald Henderson, insisted on a revolutionary design, with armoured hangars and flight decks. His reasoning was that the lack of modern, robust fighter aircraft exposed Royal Navy carriers to superior land-based air forces, and the aircraft should therefore be protected by armour during enemy air attack, leaving air defence to the carrier's guns. This ignored two factors, the inability of guns alone to defend ships, and the deterrent effect of a combat air patrol, which would at least break up enemy formations. In practice, the armoured box hangar required a 7.62cm (3in) roof and 11.4cm (4.5in) side armour, while eight pairs of 11.4cm guns and a number of light multiple guns were provided to defend the ship against enemy dive-bombing.

Despite the complexity of the design, Henderson pushed it through in only three months, and the *Illustrious* and *Victorious* were laid down early in 1937, for launching in 1939. Two more ships of the same type were ordered under the 1937 Estimates, the *Formidable* and *Indomitable*, but to remedy the small aircraft complement of the first two ships (only 36) the *Indomitable* was redesigned with a lower half-hangar. To compensate for the additional weight the hangar roof was lowered from 4.9m to 4.27m (16ft to 14ft) and its side armour was reduced in thickness.

FRENCH LEAVE IT TOO LATE

Plans to build two more under the 1938 and 1939 Estimates were shelved when the British Government invoked the 'Escalator' clause in the naval treaties to allow the Royal Navy to match the 27,433-tonne (27,000-ton) limit claimed by the US Navy and the Japanese. The aim was to produce an armoured equivalent of the *Ark Royal*, with two full-length hangars, a capacity for 72 aircraft, and more powerful machinery. This should have been an excellent solution, but the *Implacable* and *Indefatigable* were in practice less successful than the *Illustrious* class. For

one thing, they were delayed by wartime shortages until 1944, and for another, the hurried preparation of the design had introduced several bad features. There was insufficient space for the extra engineering complement to man the enlarged machinery and the extra maintainers needed to service the bigger air group. As a result, the forward half of the lower hangar had to be used for accommodation, so the new carriers were no more efficient than the original ships.

The French made a belated effort to improve their naval air arm, but they left it too late. In 1935 the French Navy had looked at proposals to convert the fast but weakly armoured heavy cruisers *Duquesne* and *Tourville* to carriers. Mercifully the proposals were vetoed, as the three schemes proposed would have resulted in air groups of only 12 to 14 aircraft, turning them from indifferent cruisers into useless carriers. Under the 1938 Programme two 18,289-tonne (18,000-ton) carriers were ordered, to be named *Joffre* and *Painlevé*. They were to have two hangars, a heavy battery of twin 12.9cm (5.1in) anti-aircraft guns and a complement of 40 aircraft, while the 200m (655ft) flight deck was offset to port. The island

Below: A tiny dockyard paddle tug nudges the gigantic HMS *Ark Royal* away from the jetty in Portsmouth Dockyard in 1938.

superstructure was very large, resembling that of a cruiser. On the modest dimensions there could be no heavy armour, only crowns for the magazines and a thin 10.2cm (4inh) belt on the waterline. The *Joffre* was laid down in November 1938 but was only 28 per cent complete when Germany invaded France. Her sister *Painlevé* had not been laid down, and all mate-

rial was destroyed, apart from the *Joffre*'s main machinery, which was completed in 1946 to power a generating station in the arsenal at Brest.

In 1935 Hitler's new *Kriegsmarine* had its first air-craft carrier authorised, the *Graf Zeppelin*, and she was launched in December 1938. A second carrier, allocated the name *Peter Strasser*, was authorised in

Left: The USS *Yorktown* (CV.10) passes through the Panama Canal on 11 July 1943, on her way back to the Pacific Ocean.

type of aircraft intended to fly from the carriers. Nor had the German Navy any experience of building or operating carriers, and the 23,369-tonne (23,000-ton) design was a hotchpotch of other navies' ideas, some old, some new, some good and some bad. Light splinter-proof protection was provided for the flight deck, as well as heavier armour on the hangar deck, and a shallow 10.2cm (4in) waterline belt. Armament was heavy: 16 15cm (5.9in) low-angle guns in casemates and six twin 10.5cm (4.1in) anti-aircraft mountings. She was grossly overpowered, with machinery developing 149,140kW (200,000hp) for a speed of 34 knots, but carried only 40 aircraft.

ENTER THE *HORNET*

The United States was still officially committed to isolationism, preferring to leave Europe to deal with its dictators, but in May 1938 Congress passed the Naval Expansion Act. It provided for 40,642 tonnes (40,000 tons) of new carrier construction, taking advantage of the expiry of the 1930 naval treaty. The United States was permitted to build to a limit of 27,433 tonnes (27,000 tons), but was still limited to a total of 177,809 tonnes (175,000 tons), so the General Board decided to order CV.8 as a repeat of the *Yorktown* design to allow time to design a new 27,433-tonne (27,000-ton) design. She was named *Hornet* and was authorised only five days after the commissioning of the USS *Enterprise*, being launched in September 1939, the month World War II broke out.

The decision to order the *Hornet* was right, not only because it gave time to prepare a carrier design which would outclass anything else in the world, but because it produced another fast carrier in time for war against Japan. In June 1939 BuC&R produced a set of Ship's Characteristics for the future CV.9 and her successors, which in turn led to sketch designs CV.9A to CV.9F, produced between July 1939 and January 1940. The choice was the same one which had bedevilled carrier design for 20 years: whether to build a large number of less battleworthy carriers which relied on other ships for protection, or to build big ships with big air groups, constituting a major offensive weapon in its own right. It must also be remembered that both the Americans and the British were trying to find cost-effective solutions on small

1939, but little work was done on her before the outbreak of war. The Royal Navy's problems with the RAF were minimal when compared to the rivalry between the *Kriegsmarine* and the *Luftwaffe*. The reserved Admiral Raeder was no match for the bombastic Reichsmarschall Goering when it came to court politics, and there were endless arguments over the

Above: The unusual stern of the new carrier HMS *Ark Royal*, with its massive overhang to provide maximum flight deck length.

Below: The Italian *Aquila*, converted from a large liner, was never actually completed, and was sunk in German hands.

AQUILA
Displacement: 28,810 tonnes (28,356 tons)
Length: 231.5m (759ft 6in)
Beam: 29.4m (96ft 5in)
Height: 7.3m (24ft)
Propulsion: Four shaft geared turbines

Speed: 32 knots
Armament: Eight 13.5cm (5.3in) guns
Crew: 1165 and 24 air personnel
Aircraft: 36

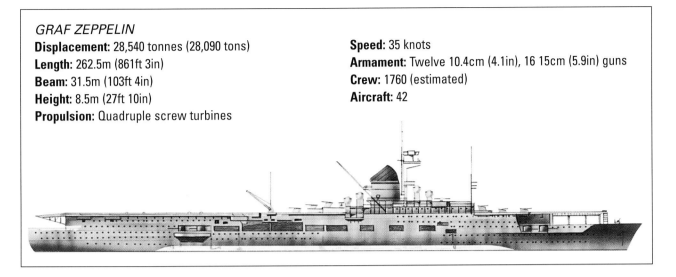

GRAF ZEPPELIN
Displacement: 28,540 tonnes (28,090 tons)
Length: 262.5m (861ft 3in)
Beam: 31.5m (103ft 4in)
Height: 8.5m (27ft 10in)
Propulsion: Quadruple screw turbines

Speed: 35 knots
Armament: Twelve 10.4cm (4.1in), 16 15cm (5.9in) guns
Crew: 1760 (estimated)
Aircraft: 42

budgets, planning for war but lacking the political support needed to defend national interests.

As we know, the US eventually opted for the big carrier, a decision which influenced the outcome of World War II as much as any made that decade. The prime requirement from the navy was to increase the number of aircraft carried, while improving speed and protection. This resulted in a rapid escalation from the 20,727-tonne (20,400-ton) CV9.A to the 25,501-26,417-tonne (25-26,000-ton) CV.9E and CV.9F, and left the *Yorktown* design far behind:

	CV.5	**CV.9F**
Displacement	20,118te (19,800t)	26,417te (26,000t)
Length	232m (761ft)	250m (820ft)
Beam	25m (83ft)	27.7m (91ft)
Draught	6.6m (21ft 9in)	8m (26ft 6in)
Power (kW)	89,484	111,855
Speed (knots)	33	35
Aviation fuel	178,000g	220,000g
Aircraft	81	90

As the Royal Navy was finding, increasing the size of the air group brought in its wake a host of new problems, none of them minor. A mere 10 per cent increase in the size of the air group called for 10 per cent more deck area. Bigger and heavier aircraft needed more fuel, and the increased fuel and ordnance required more armour to protect it, even if heavier enemy weapons did not dictate a heavier scale of protection. Bigger aircraft needed bigger lifts and more powerful catapults, as well as improved flight deck refuelling equipment. In fact the designers soon realised that even to operate the same number of aircraft as the *Yorktown* class with the same efficiency would require a bigger carrier. And acting as a longstop against any temptation to keep expanding size was the US Navy's need for its ships to pass through

Above: The *Graf Zeppelin*'s design was flawed, and arguments about her planned air group were in the end never resolved by the Germans.

the Panama Canal, effectively limiting large vessels to a beam of 33m (108ft).

The final decision to be made during the design process of CV.9 concerned the theatre in which the next war would be fought. For the United States this was simplified by the fact the British were no longer regarded as a likely enemy. Fighting in the Pacific put a premium on range, but seakeeping was also important; an endurance of 27,780km (15,000 naut. miles) at 15 knots was stipulated. Something had to give if the balance of the design was to be maintained, and so the requirement for 35 knots dropped to 33 knots and the air group was left at 80 aircraft. A requirement to carry additional engines and knocked-down airframes equivalent to 50 per cent of the air group was dropped to 25 per cent.

The final design for CV.9 worked out at 27,535 tonnes (27,100 tons), but by the summer of 1940 Congress had abandoned the statutory limit by passing the 11 Per cent Fleet Expansion Bill and the Two-Ocean Navy Bill. The former authorised three *CV.9* type, the latter approved eight more. Although they would not be ready for another two years, they were to be the weapons which destroyed Japan. Their names included some of the proudest in American history: *Essex* (CV.9), *Bonhomme Richard* (CV.10), *Intrepid* (CV.11), *Kearsage* (CV.12), *Franklin* (CV.13), *Hancock* (CV.14), *Randolph* (CV.15), *Cabot* (CV.16), *Bunker Hill* (CV.17), *Oriskany* (CV.18) and *Ticonderoga* (CV.19). Many would be renamed before completion in honour of ships lost in World War II.

CHAPTER FIVE

Baptism of Fire

Though Britain was on the defensive during the early years of World War II, at sea the carriers of the Royal Navy achieved some notable victories, such as the raid on Taranto and assisting in the sinking of the German battleship *Bismarck*. The latter triumph was the shape of things to come, and signalled the beginning of the end of the maritime supremacy of the battleship.

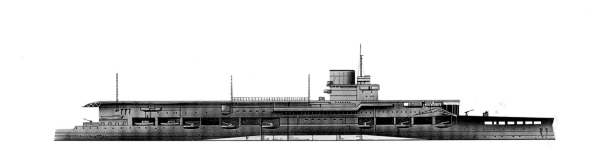

When the British ultimatum to Germany expired on 3 September the strategic position remained very much what it had been in August 1914. The Home Fleet was based at Scapa Flow in the Orkneys, guarding against a breakout by the *Kriegsmarine* into the Atlantic, and defence of the Mediterranean was largely left to the French Marine Nationale. The major difference was in the air, and there were many who looked to German air power together with submarines to wipe out the traditional British advantage of a superior fleet. Italy was neutral but could almost be guaranteed to enter the war as an ally of Germany.

First events seemed to bear out this view. In a misguided attempt to take the offensive to the U-boats

Left: HMS *Illustrious* with Fairey Albacores (wings folded) ranged on deck, and a Seafire on an outrigger ahead of the island.

the Admiralty formed 'hunting groups', with the *Ark Royal*, *Courageous*, *Furious* and *Hermes*, each escorted by four destroyers, detached from the Home Fleet to patrol in the Western Approaches and other likely areas. The idea was to support any convoys attacked by U-boats, but it had two fatal flaws. First, the Royal Navy had too few carriers to risk them in submarine-infested waters, and second, their aircraft were only equipped with an ineffective anti-submarine bomb.

On 14 September HMS *Ark Royal* was operating west of the Hebrides when her lookouts spotted torpedo-tracks passing astern. Her destroyers pounced quickly and blew *U.39* to the surface with depth-charges, but the new carrier had been very lucky. Three days later HMS *Courageous* paid the penalty when *U.29* sent her to the bottom with three torpedoes, drowning her captain and 518 of her crew.

Above: A Fairey Swordfish perched on the after-lift of HMS *Ark Royal* in 1939 or 1940, judging by the censor's handiwork.

The remaining carriers were immediately withdrawn, but the damage had been done. The loss of a large carrier was serious, considerably more so than the much-publicised torpedoing of the old battleship *Royal Oak* a month later.

The Admiralty had other problems. Two large German raiders, the 'pocket-battleships' *Admiral Graf Spee* and *Deutschland*, had slipped out into the Atlantic a week before the outbreak of war, and threatened to wreak havoc on the trade-routes. The *Deutschland* returned to Germany after sinking only two merchant ships, but the *Graf Spee* disappeared into the South Atlantic. The response was to set up eight hunting groups with the French Navy, three of them based on aircraft carriers:

Group I – operating off Ceylon (Sri Lanka), with HMS *Eagle* and two cruisers.

Group K – operating off Pernambuco, with HMS *Ark Royal* and the battlecruiser HMS *Renown.*

Group L – operating out of Brest, with the *Béarn*, the battlecruiser *Strasbourg* and three cruisers.

In addition HMS *Furious* and capital ships were sent to Halifax to cover convoys from Canada, and HMS *Glorious* went through the Suez Canal to the Indian

Ocean. None of the carriers sighted the *Graf Spee*, but the imagined proximity of the *Ark Royal* and *Renown* was one of the factors which persuaded Hitler to order the raider to scuttle herself off Montevideo after the inconclusive Battle of the River Plate in December.

The German invasion of Norway in April 1940 marked a sharp change in the tempo of the war at sea, and although the losses incurred by the German Navy seemed poor compensation for the Royal Navy's losses, they were to prove decisive. The badly managed campaign gave the Fleet Air Arm's aircrews a great deal of valuable experience. The first to go into battle was HMS *Furious*, which had sent her air group ashore for intensive training, but she sailed from the Clyde with two Swordfish squadrons on 9 April, two days after the invasion. Two days after that her aircraft carried out an unsuccessful attack on a destroyer off Trondheim and the next day they also attacked shipping at Narvik and reconnoitred the fjord for an impending surface attack by destroyers.

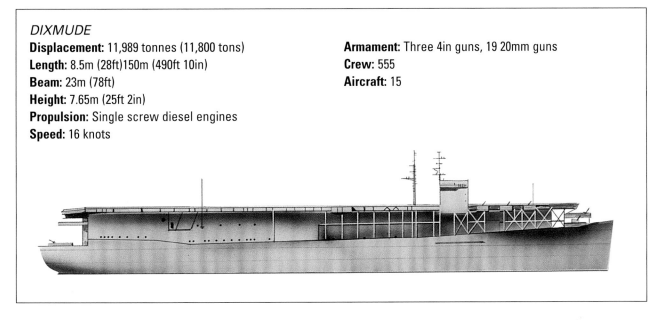

DIXMUDE
Displacement: 11,989 tonnes (11,800 tons)
Length: 8.5m (28ft)150m (490ft 10in)
Beam: 23m (78ft)
Height: 7.65m (25ft 2in)
Propulsion: Single screw diesel engines
Speed: 16 knots

Armament: Three 4in guns, 19 20mm guns
Crew: 555
Aircraft: 15

HMS *Ark Royal* had been sent to the Mediterranean in March after a short refit, and was at Alexandria with HMS *Glorious* on 10 April, when orders came to rejoin the Home Fleet. The 'Ark' had left 15 of her Skua fighter/dive-bombers behind in the Orkneys when she left for the Mediterranean, and on 10 April they sank the light cruiser *Königsberg* at Bergen with three 227kg (500lb) bombs. The luckless cruiser was the first warship to be sunk by aircraft alone. HMS *Ark Royal* and HMS *Glorious* sailed for Norway on 23 April to relieve HMS *Furious*, which was hampered by her lack of fighters.

The operations in Norway were testing. With only the most primitive navigation aids, the aircrews had to fly over mountains, dodge electric cables strung across fjords, fly in fog and snow squalls and then return to flight decks covered in icy slush. In two weeks *Furious*' aircraft flew 38,415km (23,870 miles), dropped 18 torpedoes and 15.25 tonnes (15 tons) of bombs. Both the *Furious* and *Glorious* were also used to ferry RAF Gladiators and Hurricanes to the temporary base at Bardufoss, while the *Ark Royal* covered operations further north.

GLORIOUS GOES DOWN

The collapse of the Norwegian Campaign was inevitable because the Battle of France was already lost. On 7 June HMS *Glorious* was ordered to recover the surviving RAF Gladiators and Hurricanes from Bardufoss, and despite the fact that none was fitted with a tailhook and none of the pilots had ever landed on a carrier, all landed safely. But next day disaster befell the unlucky *Glorious*, when she was

Above: The French CVE *Dixmude* (ex HMS *Biter*) was used to ferry aircraft to Indo China. She was one of three escort carriers built in the USA for lease to Britain.

intercepted by the German battlecruisers *Scharnhorst* and *Gneisenau*. Despite a spirited defence by her two escorting destroyers she was soon hit by 27.9cm (11in) shells on the flight deck, still crowded with RAF aircraft. She caught fire and sank quickly. Only 46 were saved from the two ships.

A recent TV documentary has raised the question of why HMS *Glorious* made no attempt to fly off a torpedo-strike with her Swordfish, but the carrier had only sufficient fuel to get to Scapa Flow by the most direct route. A Swordfish strike would have been suicidal; the *Glorious* would have taken half an hour to work up to full speed, and while doing so would have had to steam towards the enemy capital ships. Her best hope was to continue on course for Scapa Flow, but she was unable to get out of range. The tragedy was made worse by the failure to institute a search for survivors, but the tactical situation was confused, to say the least. Accusations that the carrier's captain sacrificed his ship recklessly because of his wish to attend a court martial of one of his subordinates does not stand up to examination.

Five days later the *Ark Royal*'s Skuas tried to dive-bomb the *Scharnhorst* at Trondheim, followed by another raid with land-based Skuas from Hatston in the Orkneys. Neither was successful but overall the 'Ark' emerged from the Norwegian debacle with a reputation for efficiency. She had become well-known to the public, in Germany as well as Britain, as the

German propaganda broadcasts plaintively repeated the same question, 'Where is the *Ark Royal*?' As early as October 1939 a *Luftwaffe* pilot had won the Iron Cross for sinking her, and the *Völkische Beobachter* even printed a picture of the event. The question became a catch-phrase for the British public and the ship a symbol for their refusal to accept defeat.

A NEW FORCE

The *Ark Royal* returned to Gibraltar little more than a week after the Norwegian Campaign ended, to form the nucleus of a new striking force under Vice Admiral James Somerville, 'Force H'. Being a fast ship, the carrier's escort was the battlecruiser *Hood*, and the force's task was to prevent any move by the Italian Fleet into the Atlantic, and to cover the area left vulnerable by the withdrawal of the French from the alliance. France was out of the war, and under the terms of the armistice signed by Marshal Petain the force of six capital ships, a seaplane carrier, 10 cruisers and a number of powerful destroyers had withdrawn to North Africa. Here they were to be

disarmed and demobilised 'under German and Italian control'. This was an ominous phrase, given the reputation for mendacity enjoyed by Hitler and Mussolini, and it did nothing to reassure the Admiralty or the British government. Although the British might accept the word of the Navy Chief of Staff, Admiral Darlan, they doubted the ability of the fleet to resist if powerful Axis forces broke their word and seized the ships.

Whatever hindsight can tell us about this view, the British were determined to settle the issue quickly, and on 3 July, following the expiry of an ultimatum to the French commander at Mers-el-Kebir, near Oran, *Ark Royal*'s Swordfish went into action against the former ally. They were given several tasks, including spotting for the capital ships' bombardment, laying mines in the harbour entrance, and bomb- and torpedo-attacks against ships trying to escape. Two

Below: The flight deck of HMS *Ark Royal* in 1940, with the deck crane in the foreground. Note the unusually small aerofoil-shaped island.

Above: HMS *Courageous* was the first major loss suffered by the Royal Navy, torpedoed by a U-boat in the Western Approaches in September 1939.

attempts to torpedo the battlecruiser *Strasbourg* failed, but a hit on an ammunition-barge alongside her sister *Dunkerque* caused considerable damage.

While this operation was going on, HMS *Hermes* was shadowing the new battleship *Richelieu*, which had escaped from Brest to Casablanca, and from there to Dakar in Senegal. On 8 July eight Swordfish scored a single hit on the *Richelieu*, damaging her propeller shafts and steering. This was enough to put the ship out of action for a year, but this was not known in London, and so Operation 'Menace', an Anglo-Free French amphibious assault on Dakar was launched. HMS *Ark Royal* had to provide air cover because the *Hermes* had been damaged in a collision, but the task was beyond her. The Swordfish were too slow to attack defended targets in daylight, and the Skuas were outclassed by the French fighters.

On the positive side, the *Ark Royal* had demonstrated the flexibility of carriers. She was able to provide fighter cover for a convoy operation in the Western Mediterranean between the attack on Mers-el-Kebir and the assault on Dakar. With Italy now in the war it was essential to reinforce Malta, and the old *Argus* was sent to the Mediterranean with a cargo of

a dozen Hurricane fighters. They were flown off safely, while the *Ark Royal*'s Swordfish attacked targets in Sardinia and her Skuas shot down shadowers. Yet even this provocation was not enough to stir the Italian Navy to defend Mussolini's beloved *Mare Nostrum*. The presence of a hostile aircraft carrier was clearly making life uncomfortable for the Italians, so HMS *Eagle* was transferred from Singapore to join Admiral Cunningham's Mediterranean Fleet. At Alexandria she embarked three obsolete Sea Gladiator biplane fighters to supplement her 18 Swordfish torpedo-bombers, and if there was little she could do with such a small air group, Cunningham was capable of causing immense mischief with limited resources.

THE BATTLE OF CALABRIA

On 9 July the Mediterranean Fleet encountered the Italian Fleet in the Battle of Calabria, during which the hard-worked aircrews of the *Eagle* had to shadow the enemy, spot for the battleships' guns, defend their own forces against high-level bombing, and last but not least, try to attack the Italian ships. They failed to slow down the retreating Italians, who were lucky to escape with minor damage, but the determination shown by the carrier's aircrews convinced Cunningham that he could take the offensive if he had a modern carrier.

HMS *COURAGEOUS*
Displacement: 26,517 tonnes (26,100 tons)
Length: 240m (786ft 5in)
Beam: 27m (90ft 6in)
Height: 8m (27ft 3in)
Propulsion: Quadruple screw turbines
Speed: 31.5 knots

Armament: Sixteen 120mm (4.7in) guns
Crew: 1216
Aircraft: 48

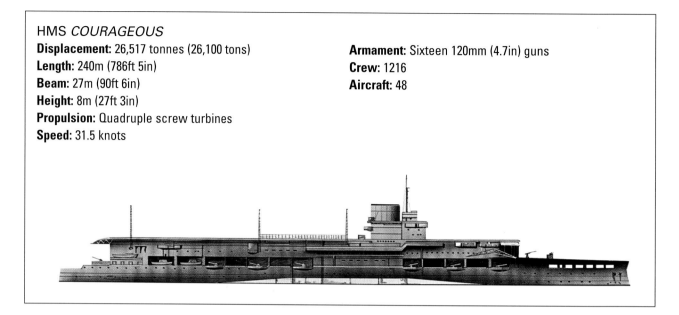

Above: HMS *Courageous* was one of the carriers that formed the backbone of the British aircraft carrier force at the outbreak of World War II. She was sunk by *U.29*.

Below: The loss of the *Ark Royal* to a single torpedo fired by *U.81* in November 1941 was the result of poor damage control.

The request to the Admiralty was granted, and on 30 August the new armoured carrier HMS *Illustrious* left Gibraltar, escorted by the battleship HMS *Valiant* and two anti-aircraft cruisers. Her air group was small, only 15 Fulmar fighters of 806 Squadron and 18 Swordfish of 815 and 819 Squadrons, but she had the benefit of one of the first production-quality Type 79Z radar. This gave her a big advantage in fleet defence as she could detect and track hostiles, giving her fighters time to gain altitude. Another improvement was long-range fuel tanks for the Swordfish, enabling them to strike at distances of up to 322km (200 miles) from the carrier. The Fairey Fulmar, although slow, had four hours' endurance and could dive at 644km (400 mph). Provided it could gain maximum height 4877m (16,000ft) it had a fair chance of shooting down Italian bombers, but could never hold its own against the enemy's fighters. In spite of their drawbacks, the Fulmars of 806 Squadron enjoyed a period of unbroken supremacy from September 1940 to January 1941, shooting down 40 Italian aircraft.

Above: HMS *Illustrious* ablaze from hits by Stuka dive-bombers off Malta in January 1941. Unlike *Ark Royal*, she reached harbour, but needed massive repairs.

Cunningham's two carriers enabled the Mediterranean Fleet to rampage through the Central Mediterranean, bombing airfields, hitting shipping between Italy and North Africa, and laying mines in harbours. All this was achieved at a small loss, but even more important was the fact that not a single major Royal Navy warship was hit by a daylight air attack. Cunningham regarded these successes as mere pinpricks, and he and his Staff were eager to launch an updated version of the 1919 plan for a torpedo-strike against the Italian Fleet in harbour. Codenamed Operation 'Judgement', the plan was to attack Taranto on Trafalgar Day, 21 October 1940. This had to be postponed when a fire broke out in the *Illustrious'* hangar, fortunately at a time when her air group had been flown ashore for maintenance, and *Eagle's* fuel-supply also started to give trouble, a legacy of earlier damage from near-misses. The damage to *Illustrious*

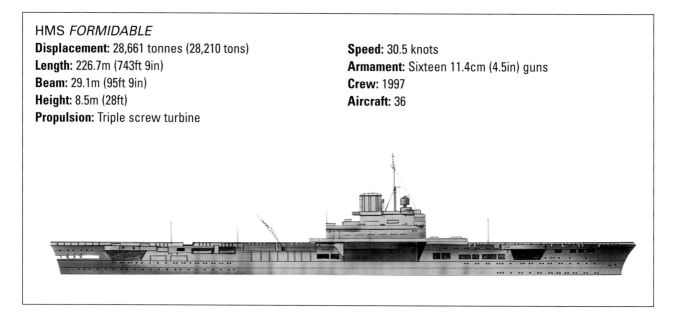

HMS *FORMIDABLE*
Displacement: 28,661 tonnes (28,210 tons)
Length: 226.7m (743ft 9in)
Beam: 29.1m (95ft 9in)
Height: 8.5m (28ft)
Propulsion: Triple screw turbine

Speed: 30.5 knots
Armament: Sixteen 11.4cm (4.5in) guns
Crew: 1997
Aircraft: 36

was not serious, and so it was decided to transfer five Swordfish and eight crews from the *Eagle* to strengthen her air group for the attack. With another Swordfish from the shore pool, the carrier could muster a total of 22 Swordfish, 14 Fulmars and four Sea Gladiators for the attack, now scheduled for the night of 11/12 November.

OPERATION 'JUDGEMENT'

In the end, only 21 Swordfish took off for the attack, in two waves an hour apart. Despite claims to the contrary, the defenders were not taken by surprise when the first six Swordfish arrived over Taranto harbour, and they were met by heavy flak, which threatened to rip the aircraft to pieces. But the attack was well coordinated, with flares dropped to illuminate the anchorage and dive-bombing of subsidiary targets to create a diversion. Two 45.7cm (18in) torpedoes ripped into the new battleship *Littorio* and a third hit the *Conte di Cavour*. An hour late the second wave of eight aircraft arrived, hitting the *Littorio* with a third torpedo and damaging another battleship, the *Duilio*. The diversionary attacks were also successful, setting fire to the oil storage tanks and wrecking the seaplane base.

The shallowness of the Taranto harbour meant that the stricken battleships could be salved and repaired, but the powerful *Littorio* was out of action for more than six months, and the *Duilio* for eight, while the *Conte di Cavour* proved too badly damaged to be worth repairing, all for the cost of 11 torpedoes and the loss of two Swordfish (one crew was saved). Italian morale suffered a shattering blow, and the

Above: HMS *Formidable* was built with protection against air attack in mind. Her hangar was set in an armoured box intended to be safe against 227kg (500lb) bombs.

Right (top): HMS *Formidable* returning from the Pacific in February 1946. Despite her impressive appearance, she had been badly damaged and was never repaired.

Right (bottom): HMS *Victorious* in the Pacific in 1943, operating temporarily under US Navy control to make up the losses in carriers since 1942.

surviving heavy units were withdrawn to more northerly bases, to be handled with great caution on the few occasions they were allowed out to sea. Coming at a time when Britain was under heavy air attack and the spectre of a German invasion was only beginning to recede, Taranto was a great boost for British morale. At a critical stage it tightened Cunningham's grip on the Mediterranean, and marked a strategic setback for the Axis which would ultimately prove fatal.

The benefits of Taranto were soon felt. On 27 November 'Force H' met the Italian Fleet off Cape Spartivento, with two of the battleships which had escaped damage during the torpedo-strike. The British were initially in a tricky situation, with a convoy passing through to Malta and the covering heavy forces divided. HMS *Ark Royal* flew off three strikes to slow the Italians down, and although they proved unsuccessful, Admiral Campioni decided to withdraw. Although this was disappointing to Admiral Somerville because he had missed a

chance to bring the reluctant Italians to battle, and also because the *Ark Royal*'s aircrews were still short of vital practice, it was nevertheless a dismal failure for the Italians.

THE FIRST RULE OF CARRIER DEFENCE

The pressure from the Mediterranean Fleet and 'Force H' was now so severe on the Italians that their German allies were forced to lend a hand. During the Norwegian Campaign a special force of Ju-87 Stuka dive-bombers had been formed to attack shipping. Known as *Fliegerkorps X*, the group had learned from its experience, and it was moved to Sicily with the specific task of sinking the *Illustrious*. What followed was an fine example of a coordinated attack catching the defenders off-balance. When the carrier was sighted about 88km (55 miles) west of Malta on 10 January 1941 a pair of Italian Savoia-Marchetti SM-79 bombers made a feint attack to draw off the combat air patrol of four Fulmars. The British pilots took the bait and pursued the Italians for 30km (20 miles), before their controller in the carrier's operations room realised that another attack was developing, in the opposite direction and at an altitude of 3657m (12,000ft). Although another four Fulmars were 'scrambled', they had no hope of countering this new threat, the Ju-87R Stukas of *Stukagruppe* 1 and the Ju-87Bs of *Stukagruppe* 2. The first rule of carrier defence had been broken: never send the whole combat air patrol after an unimportant target,

Above: Although HMS *Ark Royal* had many experimental features incorporated into her design, the shape of future British carriers was already emerging.

especially when only 104km (65 miles) from the enemy coast.

The *Illustrious* paid dearly for her over-confidence. Within 10 minutes, six bombs of various sizes hit her, three forward and three aft. The hits forward did relatively little damage, but two of three hits aft nearly sank her, hitting the after lift and starting major fires in the hangar. With her steering gear crippled the *Illustrious* was a sitting duck for further attacks, but her armoured deck had limited the extent of the damage, and when her steering was repaired she was able to set a course for Malta. The fires continued to burn and the engine-rooms filled with smoke, but she worked up to 18 knots and even managed to avoid further air attacks.

Covered by a heavy anti-aircraft barrage from the escorting battleships *Valiant* and *Warspite*, the battered carrier limped into Grand Harbour that night. The fires were not finally extinguished until five hours later, by which time 126 of her crew were dead and 91 wounded. Even so, she suffered only slight damage while lying alongside Parlatorio Wharf, allowing the dockyard staff to make her seaworthy once more. In a strange way, the battered civilians of Malta identified with the fate of their troublesome guest, and instead of blaming the carrier for the number of bombs dropped on Valletta, felt that if the *Illustrious* survived the bombing, so would they. She was ready for the break-out by 23 January, and left for Alexandria, before going through the Suez Canal on her way to the United States for full repairs. The naval base at Norfolk, Virginia, undertook the massive repairs needed, virtually rebuilding a third of her structure.

A VITAL CHANCE

The Mediterranean Fleet now faced the might of the *Luftwaffe* and the *Regia Aeronautica* without an armoured carrier, but hope was at hand. The second of the class, HMS *Formidable*, had completed her work-up, and on 10 March she passed through the Suez Canal into the Eastern Mediterranean. Cunningham was at sea on 28 March, hunting for the Italians once more, when a sighting report indicated that the Italian Fleet was itself at sea. That afternoon came the exhilarating news that one of the *Formidable*'s Albacore bombers had scored a torpedo-hit on the battleship *Vittorio Veneto*, cutting her speed to eight knots.

BATTLE OF CAPE MATAPAN

Here was the chance Cunningham had been seeking for nearly 12 months, and he pushed his ships forward at top speed, hoping to catch the crippled battleship. What he did not know was that the crew of the *Vittorio Veneto* had made some essential repairs, and her speed had risen to 19 knots, but at dusk an Albacore had torpedoed the heavy cruiser *Pola*. The efficiency of the carrier's Fulmars meant that Admiral Iachino had received no news of the whereabouts of Cunningham's fleet, so he felt safe in ordering the heavy cruisers *Fiume* and *Zara* to turn back with an escort of two destroyers to find their sister and tow her home. In the resulting Battle of Cape Matapan, during the night of 28/29 March all three cruisers were sunk by the guns of Cunningham's battleships. The victory was due above all to the efforts of the *Formidable*'s aircrews, who had accomplished all that was asked of them. They had found and immobilised enemy heavy units, defended their own fleet and denied vital intelligence to the enemy.

Matapan was to be the zenith of British carrier operations, for events were already in train that would all but sweep the Royal Navy from the Mediterranean. HMS *Formidable* was badly damaged in the evacuation from Crete, this time by Stukas flying from North African airfields. Her damage was less extensive than her sister *Illustrious*, but it was

Above: HMS *Implacable* with a Seafire parked close to the after-lift. She and her sister were not completed until 1944.

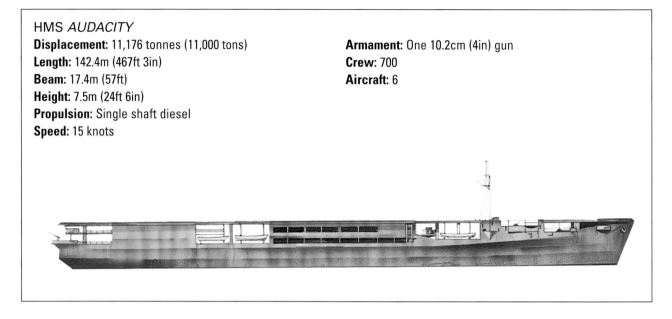

HMS *AUDACITY*
Displacement: 11,176 tonnes (11,000 tons)
Length: 142.4m (467ft 3in)
Beam: 17.4m (57ft)
Height: 7.5m (24ft 6in)
Propulsion: Single shaft diesel
Speed: 15 knots

Armament: One 10.2cm (4in) gun
Crew: 700
Aircraft: 6

beyond the capacity of the dockyard at Alexandria to repair, and she too headed for the United States. It is useless to speculate on what might have been achieved if either of the armoured carriers had not suffered heavy damage, because the chronic shortage of spares and lack of suitable aircraft meant that none of the three modern Mediterranean carriers had been able to exploit their full capabilities. The true price of the decades of dual control was now self-evident.

While HMS *Formidable* was taking part in the disastrous attempt to hold Crete, events had taken an even more serious turn in the North Atlantic. On 22 May news was received in London that the new battleship *Bismarck* had sailed from Bergen, heading for the shipping lanes of the North Atlantic. Immediately the new armoured carrier *Victorious*, which had just embarked a load of RAF Hurricanes for Malta, was told to prepare for a torpedo-strike at utmost speed. The only aircraft available were nine Swordfish of 825 Squadron and six Fulmars of 800 Squadron. She could have embarked a squadron of Albacores stationed in the Orkneys, but the local RAF Coastal Command officer refused to release them – another example of poor inter-service cooperation.

THE HUNT FOR *BISMARCK*

HMS *Victorious* had been intended as a stopgap, but on 24 May news came through that the *Bismarck* and her escorting heavy cruiser, the *Prinz Eugen*, had sunk the battlecruiser HMS *Hood* and had eluded HMS *Prince of Wales*. Although the *Bismarck* was losing oil via two underwater hits from the *Prince of Wales*, this was not known to the Home Fleet, and

Above: HMS *Audacity* had a short life as the Royal Navy's first escort carrier (CVE), but she was a great success and proved the worth of the escort carrier concept.

Victorious and her Swordfish were seen as the only hope of slowing the German battleship down. At about midnight the nine Swordfish found their quarry, and despite their lack of training, the aircrews succeeded in scoring a single torpedo-hit amidships. Even more amazing was their success in landing back on the carrier, but it was all in vain, as the 45.7cm (18in) torpedo lacked sufficient power to penetrate the *Bismarck*'s thick main armour belt.

There was only one card left to play. HMS *Ark Royal* and the battlecruiser HMS *Renown* had sailed from Gibraltar as soon as Admiral Somerville heard of the *Bismarck*'s break-out, so that his ships could prevent her from breaking away to Brest. As soon as an RAF Coastal Command Catalina sighted the *Bismarck* and her long oil slick on 26 May the *Ark Royal* was ordered to launch a torpedo-strike. What followed was a near-tragedy; the first strike of 15 Swordfish mistook the cruiser HMS *Sheffield* for the *Bismarck* in poor visibility, and launched their torpedoes. Thankfully, these were all fitted with a new duplex exploder, designed to detonate on contact or when the target's magnetic field was at its maximum strength. In the high seas, the torpedoes plunged so wildly that their magnetic exploders were set off by

Right: HMS *Indefatigable* in the Suez Canal on her way to the Pacific. Despite her impressive appearance, she was limited to operating Seafire fighters.

Above: The Merchant Aircraft Carrier (MAC ship) *Empire McAndrew* had only rudimentary facilities.

the earth's magnetism. The *Sheffield* knew that she had been wrongly targeted and managed to dodge several, and signalled to the carrier that several others of the 11 dropped had exploded on hitting the water. A second strike was ordered. This time the torpedoes' exploders were set to 'contact', and the *Sheffield* was able to assist in directing them towards the *Bismarck*.

This time the Swordfish made no mistakes, and they picked up the German battleship on their own radar. The weather was even worse than it had been during the *Victorious* strike, with low cloud and very poor visibility, and so the Swordfish attacked individually. Despite a barrage of anti-aircraft fire from 68 guns ranging from 20mm (.78in) calibre up to 10.4cm (4.1in) the biplanes lumbered on, seeming in some cases to fly almost into the *Bismarck*'s superstructure. The bravery of their crews was rewarded, and 13 torpedoes were dropped; one hit on the main armour and did little damage, but the second hit right aft and wrecked the rudders. This single hit

sealed the doom of the *Bismarck*, and although another strike was in the air, it stayed clear while the Home Fleet pounded the famous German battleship and finally sank her with torpedoes.

The *Ark Royal* returned to the Mediterranean, where she fought in the repeated battles to get aircraft and supplies through to Malta. When her luck finally ran out, it was almost an anti-climax. On 13 November 1941 she was less than 80km (50 miles) from Gibraltar when *U.81* evaded the radar and struck her on the starboard side with a single torpedo. She took a heavy list to port, but being a modern ship with good sub-division, there was every reason to think that she could be towed to Gibraltar. Flooding in the central boiler-rooms, however, put the main electrical switchboard out of action, by which time all the key electrical ratings had left the ship and were ashore in Gibraltar. As power failed, the pumps were unable to keep pace with the flooding, and next day the list had increased to such an extent that she was clearly doomed.

The loss of the 'Ark' was a shock to the British, as it revealed unsuspected weaknesses, not in the design of carriers, but in damage control procedures. A searching enquiry identified the shortcomings, and they were not repeated, but this loss and others brought to an end the brilliant string of victories in the Mediterranean, often against heavy odds. The bitter lesson of 1942 was that without modern carriers and adequate aircraft the Mediterranean was almost untenable. During the great 'Pedestal' convoy battle in August 1942 the *Indomitable* was badly damaged by bombs and the gallant old *Eagle* was torpedoed.

THE AMERICANS ARRIVE

Even the worst moments do not last, and in November 1942 the *Formidable* and *Victorious* provided cover for the Anglo-American 'Torch' landings in North Africa, as part of a much stronger 'Force H'. In 1943 the carriers remained on the offensive, covering the landings in Sicily and Italy, forcing Italy out of the war. At last the fleet carriers were freed for offensive operations in other theatres, notably Northern Norway and the Far East. The entry of the United States into the war in December 1941 finally solved the problems of the Fleet Air Arm, with at first a trickle of modern high-performance carrier aircraft which later swelled to a torrent. The first was the Grumman Wildcat, known to the Fleet Air Arm as the Martlet, and by 1944 such advanced aircraft as the TBF Avenger torpedo-bomber and the F-4U Corsair were available in large numbers. For most of the war the British aircraft industry was geared to the demands of the RAF, and as a result the Royal Navy had to put up with a mixture of adapted land aircraft such as the Sea Hurricane and the Seafire (a modified Spitfire) and dubious new types such as the Barracuda torpedo-bomber. In theory the Seafire provided the high performance needed for fleet defence, but it was too fragile for the rigours of carrier operations. Its alloy skin was liable to separate from the frames, and tail-sections were often wrenched in heavy landings. The Barracuda was a truly unlovable dive- and torpedo-bomber, slow and tricky to handle, and its shortcomings inspired a number of ribald songs and verses by the Fleet Air Arm.

After the disastrous loss of HMS *Courageous* in 1939 the Admiralty never allowed the fleet carriers to

Below: HMS *Campania* was one of the few CVEs converted in British shipyards because of the shortage of mercantile hulls.

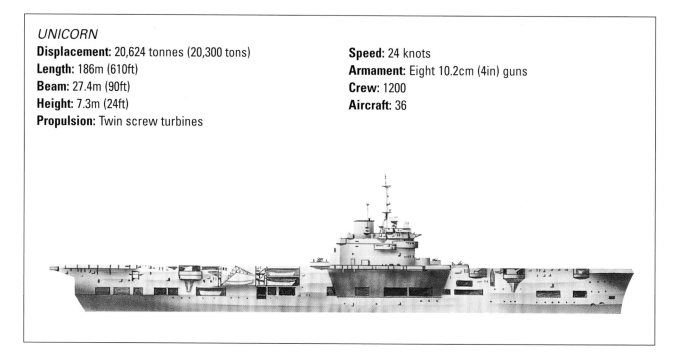

UNICORN
Displacement: 20,624 tonnes (20,300 tons)
Length: 186m (610ft)
Beam: 27.4m (90ft)
Height: 7.3m (24ft)
Propulsion: Twin screw turbines

Speed: 24 knots
Armament: Eight 10.2cm (4in) guns
Crew: 1200
Aircraft: 36

be wasted in the Battle of the Atlantic, and there were, in any case, too few to be spared. But after the German conquest of Europe in 1940 the *Luftwaffe* was able to establish bases from Norway to the Bay of Biscay, from which long-range bombers could strike at British shipping. From the autumn of 1940 Fw 200 Kondor four-engined bombers of *Kampfgruppe 40* based near Bordeaux provided sightings of convoys for the U-boats and attacked stragglers.

THE CAMSHIP

The first countermeasure was the use of the old seaplane carrier *Pegasus* (ex-*Ark Royal*) to catapult Fleet Air Arm Fulmars and Sea Hurricanes off, and in addition five merchant ships were converted. The Fighter Catapult Ship concept resembled the platforms used in the previous war, and the pilots also had to 'ditch' after each engagement, as there was no way of recovering the fighter. Although only 10 launches were made 'in anger', and only one Fw 200 was destroyed and another damaged, they were deterred, and it was sufficient to chase the shadower away. The naval ships were withdrawn by June 1942, and their place was taken by Catapult Armed Merchantmen (CAMships), flying the Red Ensign and using RAF pilots. Only eight operational launches were made by the 35 CAMships, accounting for six aircraft destroyed and three damaged, but 12 of the ships were lost while operating with the convoys.

Pre-war, the Admiralty had looked at the possibility of converting merchantmen such as large

Above: The Royal Navy's unique aircraft repair ship, HMS *Unicorn*, remembered for her role in the Korean War, was also used from time to time as a carrier.

liners to 'Trade Protection Carriers' but the shortage of aircraft had killed the concept. In late 1940 the need to protect the Gibraltar-UK convoys from air attack led to the revival of the idea, and a former German prize, the banana boat *Hannover* was selected for conversion to an 'escort carrier'. Her name, HMS *Empire Audacity*, was shortened to *Audacity* and she hoisted the White Ensign in June 1941. In September 1941 she began operations with six Martlet fighters of 802 Squadron; the hurried conversion allowed no time for luxuries such as lifts or an island, and the Martlets were parked at the after end of the flight deck. Although she made only two round trips to Gibraltar before being torpedoed in December, her aircraft proved so successful at forcing shadowing U-boats to submerge, as well as seeing off shadowers, that the Admiralty decided to order more conversions.

ESCORT AIRCRAFT CARRIERS

British shipyards proved too overworked to undertake a large-scale conversion programme, and it was to be 1944 before any more British escort carrier conversions appeared. Instead the United States was asked to fill the gap, and an order for aviation transports (AVGs) was placed with American yards, with a number allocated to the Royal Navy under the Lend-Lease Act, distinguished by the designation

BAVG. The designation was changed to Escort Aircraft Carrier (CVE), and the first entered service with the Royal Navy in September 1942.

By mid-1942 the U-boats were operating well out into the Atlantic, beyond the range of most shore-based aircraft, and in this 'Atlantic Gap' they could operate with greater efficiency, untroubled by radar-equipped aircraft. As losses mounted mid-Atlantic there was an obvious need for convoys to take their own aircraft cover with them, but, as already pointed out, there were no fleet carriers available to divert to this task.

THE MACSHIP

To bridge the gap the Admiralty ordered the conversion of several grain-carriers and oil tankers to Merchant Aircraft Carriers (MACships). The choice of these specialised bulk carriers was deliberate; their cargoes were vital, but they carried their own handling gear, which did not interfere with the flying arrangements.

Above: The CVE HMS *Pretoria Castle* was renamed *Pretoria*, and post-war was converted back to a liner, the SS *Warwick Castle*.

The deck was wide enough for a small island, and a safety barrier and three arrester wires were provided. Although the tankers had a longer deck, no lift was provided, whereas the grain-carriers had a small lift aft. The first MACship sailed in a convoy in May 1943, and by the end of the year there were 18 in service, two manned by the Dutch Navy. The only aircraft embarked were Swordfish, which were rugged enough to withstand the violent landings, but by this time they were equipped with efficient depth-charges. In the spring of 1944 they ferried over 200 aircraft to Europe for the build-up to D-Day. It was somehow appropriate that the last operational flight by a Swordfish was from the deck of the MACship *Empire Mackay* in June 1945.

CHAPTER SIX

Carriers
Rule the Waves

The Japanese attack against Pearl Harbor in December 1941 represented a milestone in the evolution of carrier warfare, and ushered in a period when Japan's fleet scored a series of stunning victories. But the US Navy did not lose its carriers at Pearl Harbor, and soon its carrier aircraft were taking the fight to the enemy, and scored a decisive victory at the Battle of Midway in June 1942.

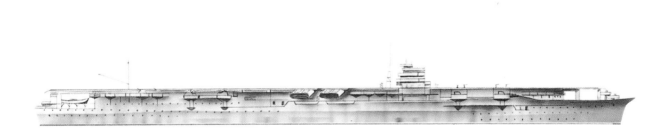

The lessons of Taranto had been studied with great interest by the Japanese. It gave them the encouragement they needed to put the finishing touches to their plans for dealing a decisive blow against the US Pacific Fleet, the main obstacle to Japanese naval expansion. The arguments for a surprise attack on the Pacific Fleet were strong. First, there was the disparity of strength, and severe attrition would have to be inflicted before the Imperial Japanese Navy could

Left: The battleships USS *West Virginia* (BB.48) and USS *Tennessee* (BB.43) ablaze after the Japanese attack on Pearl Harbor.

hope to face the US Navy on an equal footing. Second was the historical precedent of the war against Russia in 1904-05, in which the Japanese had gained a moral ascendancy over the Russians after a surprise attack. Third was the clincher, the need for a short war to prevent the United States from mustering its awesome industrial might. This last imperative relied heavily on assumptions that the Americans could be 'frightened' out of a long war by a major defeat on Day One.

Secure in their ignorance of America, the Japanese High Command proceeded with its plans. Admiral Isoroku Yamamoto, Commander-in-Chief of the Combined Fleet, was sceptical about the assumptions

75

Above: Japanese Navy 'Val' divebombers await their orders for take-off. The famous carrier *Akagi* is in the background.

made concerning America's lack of moral fibre, but he did believe that the war must be a short one, and backed plans for a surprise attack on the Pacific Fleet's main base at Pearl Harbor, Hawaii. In April and May 1940 two war-games were staged to test the feasibility of a raid by carriers. The results were conclusively favourable. Then came the news of Taranto, and the word went out to naval attachés in Rome and London to find out every detail about the attack.

Planning was entrusted to Rear Admiral Shigeru Fukudome, who brought in the Navy's most experienced pilots to devise new methods of dropping torpedoes, using wooden fins to avoid hitting the bottom of the shallow anchorage. At the same time, intelligence-gathering on American strength and fleet movements was stepped up, using consular officials in Hawaii and analysing radio-traffic. Full-scale exercises began in September 1941, and by the beginning of November Yamamoto's plans were complete, so that the breakdown of peace talks with the US Government made war inevitable. The Commander-in-Chief carried the whole Navy with him, even the cautious carrier commander, Admiral Chichi Nagumo.

As everyone knows, the attack on Pearl Harbor on 7 December 1941 was a devastating success, and Nagumo's carriers, the *Akagi*, *Kaga*, *Hiryu*, *Soryu*, *Shokaku* and *Zuikaku*, caught the US Pacific Fleet base totally unprepared. The first strike resulted in the destruction of the battleship *Arizona*, the capsizing of the *Oklahoma*, the sinking of the *California* and *West Virginia*, and varying degrees of damage to the *Maryland*, *Nevada* and *Tennessee*. The second strike destroyed large numbers of aircraft on the ground and inflicted many casualties. A third might have sunk yet more ships, but Nagumo overruled his aviators.

Fortune favours the bold, and there is no doubt that the Japanese had worked hard for their success, but however humiliating it was for the Americans, Pearl Harbor did not achieve its long-term aim. The 132 A6M2 'Zero' fighters, the 129 D3A1 'Val' dive-bombers and the 143 B5N2 'Kate' torpedo-bombers achieved rather less damage than they could have. For

Above: The Japanese carrier pilot's view of Pearl Harbor on 7 December 1941, with bombs bursting in 'Battleship Row'.

one thing, faulty intelligence meant that the US carriers *Enterprise* and *Lexington* were not caught in harbour, as planned. For another, two vital strategic targets were not even in the plan: the machine shops and the oil storage tanks. With the exception of the *Arizona*, all the battleships could be raised and repaired and the defences could be replaced, but without the oil tanks or machine shops Pearl Harbor would have been unable to support the Pacific Fleet for a year or more. More importantly, the attack brought American out of isolationism, uniting the country in a desire for revenge for the 'Day of Infamy'.

It is risky to over-simplify the history of ideas, but there can be no doubt that Pearl Harbor was a milestone in the evolution of carrier warfare. Without a classic battle fleet for at least six months, there was no possibility of the carriers being tied to a supporting role. 'Pure' carrier tactics were now the only way of taking the fight to the Japanese. The US Navy had to use the carrier task force as the core of its offensive capability, rather than the battle squadron. This idea had been envisaged and had even experimented with, but had never become official doctrine.

All this was hidden at the time, and for nearly six months after Pearl Harbor the Japanese Navy seemed unstoppable. A futile attempt to prevent Nagumo's carriers from battering Wake Island into submission was made by the *Enterprise*, *Lexington* and *Saratoga*, but it was probably fortunate that they did not meet his highly trained and supremely confident air groups so soon. Then four seaplane carriers and the *Ryujo* struck at the Philippines, but no carrier was allocated to the conquest of Malaya because the under-strength British forces had no carrier with them. The capital ships HMS *Prince of Wales* and HMS *Repulse* were sunk with ease by shore-based torpedo-bombers as they lacked even a vestige of air cover. In fact the British had planned to send HMS *Indomitable* to Singapore, but she ran aground in the West Indies. This was perhaps fortuitous as slow aircraft would have been no match for the Japanese, and she would almost certainly have swelled the total of losses.

As soon as Nagumo could get his fast carriers back into action he struck at the East Indies, attacking Rabaul in New Britain on 20 January 1942. The *Hiryu*, *Soryu* and *Zuiho* covered the invasion of Ambon, while *Ryujo*'s air group attacked the American-British-Dutch-Australian (ABDA) cruiser-force off Sumatra. On 15 February Carrier Division 1 launched a strike of 188 aircraft against Darwin and Broome in Australia; it caused havoc but it was not a prelude to invasion, merely a pre-emptive attack to deter interference with the invasion of Java. The only Allied carriers in striking distance of Java were HMS *Indomitable*, which had delivered 50 Hurricanes but had only half her air group embarked, and the USS *Langley*. The British carrier was prudently withdrawn, for her depleted air group could not have faced even the smaller *Ryujo*, but the *Langley* was caught by land-based bombers while ferrying crated P-40 fighters to Tjilatjap, and sank on 26 February. By the beginning of March, Japan had gained control of the oil, rubber and mineral wealth of South-East Asia, all at trifling cost.

JAPANESE SUPERIORITY

On 26 March the Japanese went on the rampage again, this time attacking the Royal Navy forces in the Indian Ocean. Five carriers raided the base at Trincomalee in Ceylon (Sri Lanka) and the port of Colombo, while the *Ryujo* and four cruisers went after shipping off the coast of India. On paper the Royal Navy had balanced forces, three carriers and five battleships under Vice Admiral Sir James Somerville, but the *Formidable*, *Indomitable* and *Hermes* had between them only 16 Martlets, 21 Fulmars and Sea Hurricanes, and a mixed bag of Albacores and Swordfish, facing over 100 'Zero' fighters. Nor were the battleships any sort of match for the Japanese surface fleet. These odds would tell when it came to action.

Somerville had no intention of indulging in heroics, and intended to stay out of reach by day, only closing with the enemy at night, to exploit the advantage of radar. He also had the advantage of a new secret base at Addu Atoll in the Maldive Islands, some 800km (500 miles) west-southwest of Colombo, whose existence remained unsuspected by Nagumo until much later.

The art of night-flying had been developed by the Fleet Air Arm to a much higher pitch than either the Japanese or the Americans, largely because of the limitations of its aircraft. The big convoy battles in the Mediterranean had also given the aviators valuable experience in the use of radar to improve defence against daylight attacks. The principle was to concentrate the fighters where they could do the most damage, getting them aloft to a 'holding' position, and then vectoring them out to a position at right-angles to the approaching enemy, preferably with the sun behind them. This avoided the head-on approach, with its time-consuming 180° turn in full view of the opposition. The refinement of Identification Friend or Foe (IFF) also helped the Fighter Direction Officer (FDO) to distinguish hostile from friendly aircraft on the radar plot.

A FATAL ERROR

Despite these advanced techniques, when Somerville attempted to engage Nagumo on 2 April the plan went wrong. When the Japanese carriers failed to appear at the predicted time, he over-optimistically assumed that Nagumo was withdrawing. He was wrong-footed, and allowed his Fast Division, the two armoured carriers and the battleship *Warspite*, to be detached to

Below: Zuikaku and her sister Shokaku were the most successful carriers operated by the Japanese Navy, being much larger than previous purpose-built carriers.

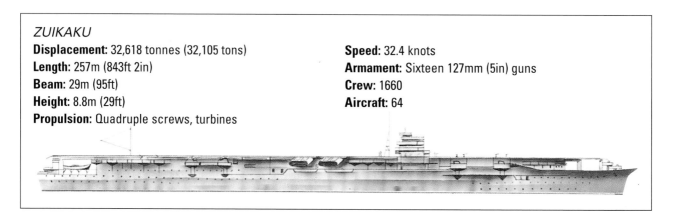

ZUIKAKU
Displacement: 32,618 tonnes (32,105 tons)
Length: 257m (843ft 2in)
Beam: 29m (95ft)
Height: 8.8m (29ft)
Propulsion: Quadruple screws, turbines

Speed: 32.4 knots
Armament: Sixteen 127mm (5in) guns
Crew: 1660
Aircraft: 64

Above: The Japanese 'Zero' fighter had no equal during the early part of the Pacific conflict, having more speed, manoeuvrability and range than Allied aircraft.

Addu to refuel. This left the *Hermes* and two destroyers dangerously exposed near Trincomalee, an error for which his force paid dearly. On 5 April the heavy cruisers *Cornwall* and *Dorsetshire* were sunk by 'Val' dive-bombers, and three days later a floatplane from the battleship *Haruna* sighted HMS *Hermes* and a number of lesser ships, and within two hours she and some of the other ships were sunk by 85 dive-bombers.

In the Central Pacific, meanwhile, American attempts to regain the initiative were getting underway. The *Yorktown* was sent through the Panama Canal early in January 1942, and joined the *Enterprise* to convoy troopships to Samoa. The Pacific Fleet now had four carriers, but on 11 January the USS *Saratoga* was damaged by a torpedo-hit southwest of Oahu, and had to return to the US for repairs. She was quickly replaced by the *Hornet*, however, so the planned raid against the Gilbert and Marshall Islands could go ahead.

The carriers were now grouped into three task forces: TF 8, built around the *Enterprise* under Rear Admiral Halsey, TF 11 under Rear Admiral Brown in the *Lexington*, and TF 17 under Rear Admiral Fletcher in the *Yorktown*. TF 8 and TF 17 were to carry out the strike, while TF 11 was to cover them from a position east of Wake Island. The first strike was by TF 8 against Kwajalein Atoll in the Marshalls, and inflicted slight damage on shipping at the cost of light casualties from the defending fighters. TF 17's strike against the Gilberts achieved even less, and the raid was later described as a 'very expensive form of pilot training'. But it did show up several weaknesses in US Navy tactics. The worst was the lack of IFF in the F4F Wildcat (the Fleet Air Arm's Martlet), which meant that FDOs had great difficulty in distinguishing even the strike aircraft from the combat air patrol. Furthermore, the lack of good long-range radios meant that two-way radio contact could not be maintained outside a range of 48km (30 miles).

The new carrier *Hornet* was earmarked for an unusual task. As early as 10 January 1942 a submariner on the staff of the Chief of Naval Operations (CNO) had suggested that Army bombers could be flown off a Navy carrier to bomb Tokyo. When the CNO's Air Operations Staff studied the idea they discovered that a B-25 Mitchell twin-engined bomber could just manage a take-off. There was no question of landing back on the carrier, and it was hoped that China could provide a landing strip. The well-known pre-war flying pilot, Lieutenant Colonel James Doolittle, was selected to lead the raid, and on 10 February the USS *Hornet* launched two B-25s in a trial off the Virginia Capes.

After frantic preparation the carrier left San Francisco on 2 April with no fewer than 16 B-25s on her flight deck. She had her sister *Enterprise* as an escort for the most dangerous part of the mission, and together they formed TF 16 under Halsey's command. For the final run the carriers left their destroyers behind as they lacked high-speed endurance, but four cruisers remained in company. On 18 April all 16 B-25s were launched safely, despite a 40-knot gale, and TF 16 withdrew at top speed.

SHANGRI-LA

The Japanese were aware of the raid, but failed to realise that B-25s were involved, and predicted the time of arrival wrongly so the defences of Tokyo were caught off-balance. The raiders escaped without being intercepted, and headed for China, but bad weather over Chungking forced many of the crews to bail-out in darkness. Four crash-landed, and the crew of one were interned at Vladivostok by the Russians. Only three aircrew were lost. The military results of the Doolittle Raid were negligible, but it marked a break in a run of American defeats, and incensed the Japanese. Pressed to reveal the 'secret base' from which the raid had been launched, President Roosevelt called it 'Shangri-la' after the James Hilton novel, and to commemorate the exploit a new *Essex* class carrier was renamed *Shangri-la*. The next major event was the Battle of the Coral Sea, which came about because Admiral Yamamoto's cherished decisive battle had not yet taken place. His strategy had worked almost perfectly so far; the US Pacific Fleet had been almost destroyed, and a chain of island bases had been established to protect Japan's new conquests. But, as the Doolittle Raid demonstrated, the US Navy's carriers were still dangerous. He had other plans to bring the Americans to battle, but acquiesced in an Army plan to clear hostile forces from the southwest Pacific. The Japanese Army recognised that Australia was vital to any Allied counter-offensive, and that any such attack would be

directed against their base at Rabaul, and so asked for Navy support. Operation 'Mo' included an amphibious assault on Port Moresby in New Guinea and the capture of Tulagi in the Solomon Islands.

The Carrier Strike Force, under Admiral Takeo Takagi and including the *Shokaku* and *Zuikaku*, left Truk on 1 May. Five days later it was in position to stop any American strike against the Port Moresby landings. The US forces included the carrier *Lexington* under Rear Admiral Aubrey W. Fitch and the *Yorktown* under Rear Admiral Frank W. Fletcher, TF 17. The Americans had a slight edge in the numbers of carrier aircraft, but above all they had the priceless benefit of superior intelligence, thanks to the cryptographers at Pearl Harbor. Admiral Nimitz and his staff knew the Japanese objectives exactly. They also had radar, and some of *Yorktown*'s fighters had just received IFF equipment. But at this stage the Japanese carrier tactics were still superior. Instead of operating each carrier as the nucleus of a separate task force, their carriers operated as a single unit, contributing maximum air cover against attack and gaining maximum benefit from the defensive firepower of the escorts. It allowed fighter patrols and strikes to be coordinated, whereas American multiple strikes tended to be more haphazard.

First blood was drawn by the US carriers, which sighted the invasion transports in Tulagi harbour and attacked on the morning of 4 May, sinking and damaging a number of ships. Two days later an Army bomber spotted the small carrier *Shoho* refuelling at Bougainville. Before noon on 7 May the *Lexington* and *Yorktown* air groups sank her with bombs and torpedoes. But the attack had revealed the presence of TF 17, and the Americans realised that this was not the Japanese Carrier Strike Force.

FIRST BLOOD

Admiral Takagi, meanwhile, was operating well to the north of TF 17, but was equally unaware of his enemy's position. Early on the morning of 7 May a sighting report indicated a carrier and a cruiser, so he ordered an all-out strike from the *Shokaku* and *Zuikaku*. They were in fact the oiler *Neosho* and her escorting destroyer, the USS *Sims*, which put up such a fight that 51 carrier bombers took two-and-a-half hours to sink them. In all Takagi lost five precious hours in this uncharacteristically inept operation, and failed in his primary mission, the location of TF 17, which was at that moment preparing to sink the *Shoho*. In a belated attempt to recover the initiative

Above: The *Akagi* at sea in mid-1941. Following her modernisation she was given a port-side island, like the newer *Hiryu*.

the Japanese launched a second strike, this time against the *Yorktown*, but an error in calculating her position led the strike astray. On the way back they were hit hard by the *Yorktown*'s CAP, losing nine aircraft. The survivors then lost their way, and four even tried to land on the *Yorktown*'s deck until they received an unpleasant surprise. The total losses were 21 out of the 27 aircraft which had taken off, amounting to 77 per cent on the first day of the battle, without even engaging the American carriers.

Takagi took his carriers northwards, while the *Yorktown* turned east to clear a patch of bad weather which was hindering flying, but during the night the Japanese reversed course. A dawn search was launched, in the hope of attacking the American carrier as soon it was located, and at 0800 hours a sighting was made. Unfortunately for Takagi, this signal was intercepted and passed to Admiral Fitch in the *Lexington,* who had already ordered a major search to start at 0625. At almost the same time a Dauntless dive-bomber spotted the *Shokaku* and *Zuikaku*, and the world's first ever carrier-versus-carrier battle was underway.

The American carriers put up a combined total of 84 aircraft, the Japanese 69. *Yorktown*'s CVG-5 struck first. *Lexington*'s CVG-2 got lost and did not attack for another hour. The CVG-5 torpedo-strike was a failure, but the 24 dive-bombers scored two hits on the *Shokaku*, one forward which started an avgas fire, and one aft, which wrecked the engine repair workshop. When the remnants of the *Lexington*'s strike arrived, they scored another bomb-hit which caused little damage.

The Japanese attack began at 1118 hours, with 51 bombers and 18 fighters operating as a single force. The raid was detected by *Lexington*'s radar at 113km (70 miles), but an error by her FDO put the CAP between the dive-bombers at 5486m (18,000ft) and the fighters and torpedo-bombers at 1828m (6000ft). Compounding the error, the Wildcats were kept too close to the carrier, and so only three fighters made contact before the attack developed. The *Yorktown*'s manoeuvrability helped her to avoid the torpedoes, but a 250kg (550lb) bomb hit inboard of the island and penetrated three decks before exploding. The less manoeuvrable *Lexington* was attacked by six torpedo-bombers, three on either side of the bow. She was hit once on the port side forward and a second time amidships, and suffered slight damage from two 60kg (130lb) bombs.

For a while the *Lexington* appeared to be holding her own, as fire parties dealt with three fires, but the avgas system had been severely damaged by the excessive 'whip' of the hull from the torpedo-detonations. Many leaks allowed avgas fumes to permeate the lower decks, and about an hour after the attack an electrical spark set off a big explosion, followed by several smaller ones and a new fire. During all this she continued to recover aircraft and even flew off a CAP, but the fires were gaining, and at 1445 hours she was shaken by a second big explosion. Half an hour later flying operations were suspended and she asked the *Yorktown* to take aboard as many aircraft as possible. After 1700 she was abandoned, to be torpedoed three hours later by an escorting destroyer.

The *Yorktown* had been lucky. Her fires were brought under control and at no time was her efficiency impaired. But the elated Japanese pilots saw her burning and reported that they had sunk *two* carriers. The *Shokaku* was badly damaged and limped home for three months of repairs. Her sister also needed repairs to defects, and so at a crucial moment in the Pacific the two best Japanese carriers were out of action. The US Navy had won an important strategic victory on Day One, and had then suffered a tactical defeat on Day Two. The invasion of Port Moresby had been stopped, but they had lost a big carrier in exchange for a small one. The Japanese aircrews had been better, but they and their aircraft were squandered recklessly.

Above: The *Hiryu* on trials in April 1939, shortly after completion. She was sunk at Midway a little over three years later.

Understandably, the Japanese regarded the Coral Sea battle as a side-show. Although the Army still wanted to capture Port Moresby as a prelude to an invasion of Northern Australia, Yamamoto and the Navy saw their most important priority as the annihilation of the US Navy's carriers. The C-in-C insisted that the small base of Midway was the key. Although just two islands totalling only 445 hectares (1100 acres), the atoll was an important advanced post almost exactly in the centre of the Pacific. In Japanese hands it would drive a wedge into the American strategic triangle which had its base on the west coast and its apex at Pearl Harbor, and Yamamoto knew that the Americans would have to deploy forces to defend it. Fighting at such a distance from Japan would pose some logistic problems, but the Combined Fleet staff knew that the chance to trap the American carriers was worth the risk.

THE BATTLE FOR MIDWAY

The plan was complex. Four fast carriers would attack Midway, with a powerful surface force backing them up. To avoid the risk of the Americans launching an attack against the Kurile Islands north of the Japanese home islands, the Aleutian Islands 2414km (1500

(1500 miles) north of Midway would be occupied. This force would be supported by two light carriers, and a covering force of a third light carrier would be positioned 805km (500 miles) southwest of the Aleutians and 1851km (1150 miles) northwest of the Midway carrier force. The plan called for a rapid occupation of Midway to allow bases for reconnaissance aircraft to be established, and so two seaplane carriers were allocated to the invasion force.

There were two snags. Everything hinged on surprise, and also on superior intelligence regarding the numbers and whereabouts of the US Navy carriers. Thanks to the Navy cryptographers, the element of surprise was already lost, and the Japanese believed that the *Yorktown* had been sunk at the Battle of the Coral Sea, and therefore calculated that they faced only two carriers. Possession of the Japanese naval codes told Admiral Nimitz that a major operation in the central Pacific was planned, and also enabled him to take measures to frustrate Japanese reconnaissance. The Japanese contributed their own measure of complacency, putting a patrol line of 13 submarines in place *after* TF 16 and TF 17 had passed on their way to Midway. They could hardly have predicted that it would take only three days to repair the *Yorktown*'s battle damage.

The Americans had been forced to make changes in their command. Rear Admiral Fletcher continued to fly his flag in the *Yorktown* as commander of TF 17, but Halsey was ill and command of TF 16 passed to Rear Admiral Raymond Spruance, flying his flag in the *Enterprise* and including the *Hornet*. Vice Admiral Nagumo's Carrier Strike Force included the

Akagi, *Kaga*, *Hiryu* and *Soryu*, but he complained that they had all been driven hard since December 1941, and badly needed refitting. Nobody took the tetchy Nagumo seriously, remembering that he had been just as pessimistic before the attack on Pearl Harbor. Yamamoto was ill, but even if he had been on top form the fatal intelligence estimate about the number of American carriers had become vital to the battle plan – odds of 3:4 were not as convincing as 2:4. The early warning of the attack had allowed Admiral Nimitz to position his carriers 643km (400 miles) northeast of Midway, and also allowed him to ignore the diversionary attack on the Aleutians.

DAWN – THE ENEMIES CLOSE IN

On 3 June a Catalina flying boat spotted the invasion force under Admiral Kondo about 1287km (800 miles) west of Midway, and that afternoon a series of attacks began by the aircraft based on Midway, most of them ineffective. By nightfall the two opposing carrier forces were approaching the island, neither aware of the other's position. The difference lay in the fact that the Americans knew they were looking for four carriers, whereas the Japanese were not even certain that any US carriers were near. At dawn on 4 June they were less than 400km (250 miles) apart, and Nagumo launched 108 aircraft for a softening-up attack on Midway's defences. Typically, he kept back *Kaga*'s air group in case any American ships were sighted, while Fletcher, equally cautious, sent only 10 SBDs to ensure that the Japanese had not turned his flank. At 0602 hours he finally learned from a Catalina that the enemy carriers had been sighted 333km (207 miles) northeast of Midway, and five minutes later he ordered Spruance to launch a strike from his two carriers. He himself would launch a strike as soon as the SBDs had returned to the *Yorktown*.

Below: The *Taiho* (Giant Phoenix) resembled the British *Illustrious* design, with a closed hangar and armoured flight deck.

TAIHO
Displacement: 37,866 tonnes (37,270 tons)
Length: 260.6m (855ft)
Beam: 30m (98ft 6in)
Height: 9.6m (31ft 6in)

Propulsion: Quadruple screw turbines
Speed: 33.3 knots
Armament: Twelve 10cm (3.9in), 71 25mm (1in) guns
Crew: 1751
Aircraft: 53

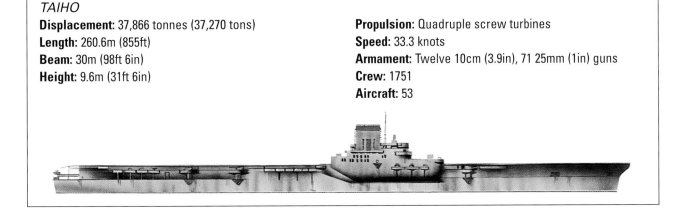

At first things did not go well. Spruance's Chief of Staff decided not to reconnoitre to confirm the sighting report, and ordered an immediate strike. It was a rash move because Nagumo had over 90 aircraft in hand, and the piecemeal attacks which developed were mauled by the Japanese carriers' CAP. At 0707 four land-based B-26 bombers and six TBF Avengers attacked *Akagi* and *Soryu*, losing seven without scoring a hit. Nagumo concluded from this attack that Midway's defences needed further bombardment, and committed 93 aircraft to the task. This meant striking down the B5Ns to the hangar and replacing their torpedoes with bombs, but just 14 minutes after the order had been given, a floatplane reported the presence of American ships. There was no mention of carriers or of the fact that aircraft were being launched, but Nagumo hesitated, asked the floatplane to confirm its report, and then suspended the rearming of the remaining bombers.

At 0755 hours Midway aircraft attacked once more, aiming for the *Hiryu* and *Soryu*. They attacked again at 0810 and a third time at 0830, achieving nothing. To make matters worse, the third attack by SB2U Vindicators coincided with the return of the first strike, and the resulting confusion resulted in crashes and ditchings. The final total was 36 aircraft lost, 33 per cent of the strike. But the attacks from Midway, however ineffective, kept up the pressure on Nagumo, and he knew that he had been outmanoeuvred. He finished recovering the aircraft and resolutely turned northwards for a strike against TF 16. Even the arrival of the *Enterprise* and *Hornet* did not deflect him, for as usual they were uncoordinated: four strikes were launched – the first was destroyed, the second and third inflicted no damage while the fourth failed to find its prey.

Another 50 SBDs had overflown the estimated position, and turned back to find the *Enterprise*, when they sighted a lone Japanese destroyer. Interpreting her movements correctly, the Air Group Commander McClusky ordered his group to follow her, and at about 1005 they sighted all four enemy carriers steaming in a diamond formation. This time the attack was properly coordinated, with *Akagi* hit by two bombs, *Kaga* hit by four more, and *Soryu* by three, with no loss suffered by the dive-bombers. The worst damage was suffered by the *Kaga*, which had the forward part of the ship set on fire and the captain killed by a hit in front of the island. She burned for about three hours before being abandoned, with 800 of her crew lost. The *Soryu* was on fire from end to end, and shortly after 1040 hours lost steering. She was abandoned five minutes later but drifted for another eight hours before sinking with the loss of over 700 men. The *Akagi* stood up better, and her captain's energetic efforts won time for Admiral Nagumo to shift his flag to a light cruiser, and she was not finally abandoned until 1915 hours losing only 221 dead.

Despite the terrible loss of three-quarters of his force, Nagumo still had a major card in his hand; the *Hiryu* was undamaged, and was immediately ordered to launch a strike. But she had lost 10 bombers in the strike against Midway, and the survivors needed repairs and servicing, so she was unable to launch a fully coordinated bomb- and torpedo-attack. The Americans had used up all but 17 of their strike aircraft and the 60 TBDs and SBDs returning would need at least four hours to rearm and refuel.

Below: The *Shinano's* profile does not give away her battleship origin, but many internal features of the *Yamato* design remained.

SHINANO

Displacement: 74,208 tonnes (73,040 tons)
Length: 266m (872ft 9in)
Beam: 40m (131ft 3in)
Height: 10.3m (33ft 9in)
Propulsion: Quadruple screw turbine

Speed: 28 knots
Armament: Sixteen 12.7cm (5in), 145 25mm (1in) guns, 336 rocket launchers
Crew: 2400
Aircraft: 120

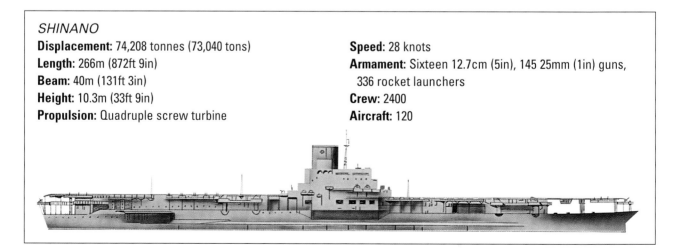

Above: The *Zuiho* under attack during the Battle of Leyte Gulf in October 1944. The camouflage scheme tried to create the illusion of a battleship.

The *Yorktown* was the only American carrier with any reconnaissance aircraft left, at 1130 hours she launched 10 SBDs before recovering her strike aircraft. Half an hour later her radar detected the *Hiryu*'s incoming strike, and her defending Wildcats were vectored out to intercept. Aboard the carrier last-minute precautions were taken; refuelling was stopped and the avgas supply system was flooded with CO2 gas to damp down the deadly vapour.

THE *YORKTOWN* IS HIT

A lethal dogfight developed over the *Yorktown*, with many of the attackers jettisoning their bombs to fight on more equal terms, but eight D3A 'Vals' did not, and streaked through the screen. Six were shot down but three bombs hit the carrier, one bursting on the flight deck, a second detonating at the base of the funnel and putting the boiler fires out, and the third penetrating three decks. The damage control was excellent, and an avgas fire below decks was contained, but

the ship lost all power and by 1220 hours lay dead in the water. Spruance detached two cruisers and two destroyers to protect the stricken carrier, and by 1320 hours three boilers were functioning and she had worked up to 20 knots. The CAP had been dispersed to the other carriers and she was able to start refuelling and arming her strike aircraft once more. After about an hour *Hiryu*'s second strike was detected, ten B5N 'Kates' and six Zeroes. This time the CAP was only able to shoot down two 'Kates', and two of the four torpedoes dropped hit the *Yorktown* on the port side. The five surviving attackers returned to report that they had sunk the carrier.

Now the Japanese intelligence errors caught up with them. The pilots could not believe that the carrier they had seen blazing at noon could have survived

(remembering what had just happened to three of their own) and assumed they had sunk a *second* carrier. As they were convinced that only two carriers were present, logically there were no more. But the *Yorktown* was still afloat, despite her heavy damage, and her sisters were undamaged, although their air groups were sadly depleted. TF 16 prepared its forlorn hope: four TBDs and 24 SBDs from the *Enterprise* and 22 SBDs from the *Hornet*. The *Enterprise* launched her strike at about 1530 hours, followed 30 minutes later by the *Hornet*'s. The 50 Wildcats were held back to protect the carriers.

The *Hiryu* had been preparing for a third strike against the *Yorktown* at 1630 but it was delayed to give the exhausted aircrews time to eat an evening meal. That meal was never finished, because without warning 13 dive-bombers attacked out of the sun, while others attacked the escorts. The first three bombs missed, but four then hit, two forward of the island and two amidships. Once again there was a searing explosion in the hangar, detonating the torpedo warheads and bombs stored in readiness for the next strike. The blast knocked out the fire-fighting equipment, and nothing could be done to stop the blaze spreading throughout the ship. She could still steam at 28 knots but the fire burned all night and she abandoned at 0230 hours.

Yamamoto took the news calmly, and tried to concentrate his scattered forces for a renewed attack. Eventually on 5 June he was forced to accept defeat and retired with the Combined Fleet and the invasion force. In any case, Spruance had taken his carriers well to the East, and there were no longer any American carriers for the Japanese to bring to action.

Nevertheless, the Japanese took a minor revenge. The battered *Yorktown* was still afloat at dawn on the 5th, and efforts were made to tow her home. At 0200 hours the next morning four destroyers were standing by. At 0400 the *Hamman* came alongside to provide power for pumps, and as the carrier's list reduced and the fires were put out hopes rose that she might be saved. But at 1330 the following afternoon the Japanese submarine *1.168* came up on her, and fired a spread of four torpedoes. Three hit the *Yorktown* on the starboard side; a fourth blew the *Hamman* apart. In spite of this the carrier did not give up the fight until 0500 hours on 7 June. Her tremendous fight was finally over.

Left: The *Amagi* lies wrecked at Kure. Like other Japanese carriers, she arrived too late to alter the outcome of the war.

CHAPTER SEVEN

Reaping the Whirlwind

Once the US Navy had gained the strategic initiative in the Pacific, her carriers were able to inflict a series of crushing defeats on the Japanese Navy. Aircraft flying from such famous vessels as the *Enterprise*, *Essex* and *Independence* destroyed the Japanese Navy's ability to wage an offensive war. And in the end helped to retake all the territories lost to Japan during the early war years.

Midway had far-reaching effects and was a turning point in the Pacific War. Although it did not win the war, it gave the Japanese High Command a severe shock, and it is said that Imperial Headquarters sank into a mood of black despair for several weeks afterwards, fearing an immediate onslaught on Japan itself. The loss of four of their most powerful carriers had been bad enough, but at least 260 aircraft had been lost as well, along with 45 per cent of their magnificent crews. Soon a fatal

Left: Hellcat dive-bombers crowd the after flight deck of a US Navy carrier in the Pacific.

rift opened up between the Army and the Navy; despite the losses the Army wanted to continue its expansion, and the generals demanded naval air support. What the carrier force needed was time to rest, train new pilots and re-equip with new aircraft. Yamamoto's worst fears became reality; the 'decisive' battle had been fought without achieving the destruction of the main enemy fleet, and now a war of rival industries had begun. The first of the new *Essex* class carriers were nearing completion, as well as a huge fleet of surface warships and submarines, all to achieve the total destruction of Japan.

There were in fact to be only two more genuine carrier-versus-carrier battles: the Battle of the Eastern Solomons on 24 August and the Battle of Santa Cruz on 26 October. They came about because the Japanese Army insisted on occupying the Solomon Islands, which precipitated the ferocious struggle for Guadalcanal. In the first battle the *Ryujo* was sunk and the *Enterprise* was damaged, and as at Midway, the American forces frustrated an attempted invasion. Then on 31 August the *Saratoga* was damaged by a torpedo from a submarine, and had to return to the United States for repairs. On 15 September the *Wasp* was also torpedoed, but this time the 'whip' of the hull ruptured avgas lines and fire mains, and she was gutted by fire. Within half an hour she had to be abandoned, leaving the *Hornet* the only carrier in the front line. Fortunately the *Enterprise* returned to duty only two days before the Santa Cruz battle. The odds were heavy as Nagumo had the *Shokaku*, *Zuikaku*, *Zuiho* and *Junyo*. Even so, the only Japanese success was to sink the *Hornet* in a textbook attack by dive- and torpedo-bombers; she might have survived but eventually she had to be scuttled to avoid capture, and the *coup de grace* was administered by Japanese destroyers, which sank her with four 'Long Lance' torpedoes.

JAPANESE LOSSES

Santa Cruz was a Pyrrhic victory for the Japanese, for although they had sunk two US carriers and had suffered in return only slight damage to the *Shokaku* and *Zuikaku*, they had lost over 100 aircraft and most of their crews in futile attrition around Guadalcanal.

When the struggle for the island petered out at the beginning of February 1943 the US Navy had lost two carriers, eight cruisers and 14 destroyers, but the Japanese Naval Air Force had lost over 1000 aircraft and many hundreds of aircrew. To make matters worse, the Japanese Navy had been pursuing no crucial strategic aim, merely supporting the Army.

The industrial war was now in top gear. Although, because of their industrial weakness, the Japanese had gambled on a short war they had made some contingency plans. As early as 1931 a large submarine depot ship had been designed for rapid conversion to a carrier, and in 1934 two large oilers were similarly earmarked. As a result the *Taigei*, *Tsurugizaki* and *Takasaki* re-emerged in 1940-41 as the *Ryuho* (13,544 tonnes [13,330 tons] and 31 aircraft), *Shoho* and *Zuiho* (both 11,443 tonnes [11,262 tons] and 30 aircraft). Three luxury liners were also converted, becoming the *Taigei*, *Chuyo* and *Unyo*, and these served as second-line carriers. Had the Japanese Navy had any coherent policy of commerce-protection they would have been the first CVEs, but they spent most of the time ferrying aircraft and training aircrew. Two 27,433-tonne (27,000-ton) liners became the *Hiyo* and *Junyo* in 1942, and their capacity of 53 aircraft made them valuable additions. A new fleet carrier ordered in 1939 was the first Japanese carrier with an armoured flight deck, but there is no evidence that the design was influenced by the British *Illustrious* class.

Below: The USS *Lexington* in her pre-war guise. In early 1942 the four twin 20.3cm (8in) gun turrets were removed.

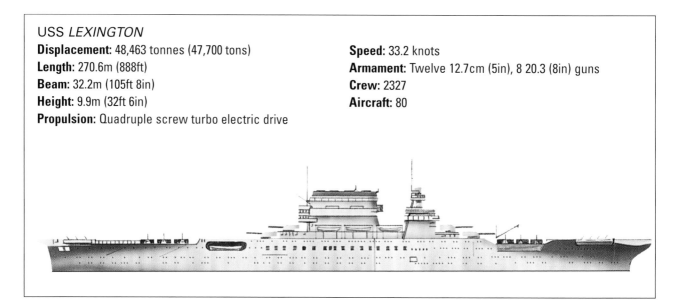

USS *LEXINGTON*
Displacement: 48,463 tonnes (47,700 tons)
Length: 270.6m (888ft)
Beam: 32.2m (105ft 8in)
Height: 9.9m (32ft 6in)
Propulsion: Quadruple screw turbo electric drive

Speed: 33.2 knots
Armament: Twelve 12.7cm (5in), 8 20.3 (8in) guns
Crew: 2327
Aircraft: 80

Named *Taiho*, she did not enter service until 1944. Two improved versions of the *Hiryu* were ordered in 1941, the *Unryu* and *Amagi*. After Midway the programmes were recast, but by then ordering 13 more of the *Unryu* class was wildly unrealistic. The most ambitious conversion of all was that of the incomplete giant battleship *Shinano*, which had been suspended in 1942 to allow more urgent ships to be built. She was completed as a support carrier rather than a fleet carrier, being intended to accept aircraft from other carriers for servicing and repair, and to refuel and re-arm them. In practice, however, a small fighter complement was added for self-defence.

Despite these remarkable efforts of improvisation, the Japanese never grasped the main problem – shortage of pilots. The pre-war flying school had turned out no more than 100 pilots a year, and even after the horrendous losses in 1942 the Navy seemed unable to speed up the process to make good the attrition. In contrast the US Navy's flying training facilities at

Above: Repair parties dealing with damage to the wooden flight deck of the USS *Yorktown* during the Battle of Midway.

Pensacola in Florida were expanded, and by mid-1943 some 45,000 pilots were 'in the pipeline'. The capacity was so huge that the Royal Navy sent its Fleet Air Arm pilots to compensate for the lack of good training facilities in wartime Britain. It soon became obvious that both navies would have more pilots than carriers for them to fly from, and urgent steps were taken to get more aircraft to sea. Even the enormous capacity of US shipyards was rapidly taken up, and measures were taken to convert other hulls. In January 1942 the first conversion of a light cruiser into a light aircraft carrier (CVL) was ordered, followed by 10 more, known as the *Independence* (*CVL.22*) class. Delivered in 1943, they were a tight squeeze, but their high speed made them suitable for supporting fleet operations.

The US Navy was, of course, fighting a two-ocean war, and was simultaneously running a CVE programme to fight in the Battle of the Atlantic. The first conversion from a standard mercantile hull had been commissioned in June 1941, and five more were built for the Royal Navy. Immediately after Pearl Harbor 25 more were ordered, 24 for the US Navy and one for the Royal Navy, and eventually the British received a total of 39. It was also recognised that these 'Woolworth carriers' were ideal for supporting amphibious operations and ferrying aircraft to distant theatres. The CVEs could be risked closer inshore than fleet carriers, to provide close air support until airstrips could be established ashore.

To simplify production the *Essex* design was repeated but lengthened by 3.66m (12ft), the so-called 'Long hull' type. Nineteen were ordered between August 1942 and June 1943, but eight were cancelled at the end of the war. In August 1942 another order was placed, for the first of three so-called 'battle carriers' or CVBs. This was the 45,722-tonne (45,000-

Above: Amid a peppering of gun blasts, the *Yorktown* takes a bomb hit while manoeuvring at speed during the Battle of Midway in June 1942.

ton) USS *Midway* (*CV.41*), the first armoured deck carrier in the US Navy. Slightly smaller than the *Shinano*, she and her sisters *Franklin D. Roosevelt* and *Coral Sea* had a nominal air group of 137 aircraft and a speed of 33 knots. Three more were cancelled in 1945.

The Royal Navy's efforts to expand its carrier force were hampered by shortages of materials and the disruptive effects of air raids on shipyards. As a result, work proceeded slowly on the 27,433-tonne (27,000-ton) *Implacable* and *Indefatigable*, and the Admiralty looked for other solutions. A useful addition was the small support or maintenance carrier *Unicorn*, which had been ordered in 1938 and launched in 1941. Plans had been drawn up in 1940 for an improved *Implacable* design, but work was shelved until 1942, giving time for war experience to

Above: The launch of the new *Lexington* (CV.16) 27,000-tonne (26,573-ton) aircraft carrier of the *Essex* class, in September 1942.

be incorporated. Four were planned, to be named *Audacious*, *Ark Royal*, *Africa* and *Eagle*, each displacing 37,391 tonnes (36,800 tons). They retained the closed hangar, but the increase in size gave a theoretical capacity of 100 aircraft. Work proceeded slowly, and at the end of the war only *Audacious* and *Ark Royal* were worth completing, *Audacious* taking the name *Eagle*.

A NEW DESIGN

The construction of large carriers could only be undertaken by the biggest yards, and to meet the desperate need for new tonnage another design was drawn up in 1941-42 for light fleet carriers. Not CVEs, they were intended to work with the fleet, and so careful consideration was given to essentials rather than luxuries. Side and deck armour was discarded to allow weight to be devoted to size, while speed was reduced to 23 knots at full load. Battle experience had shown that a damaged carrier's list soon made flying operations impossible, so the

normal 'sandwich' protection was reduced to allow the ship to settle slowly but upright. To speed construction the hull up to the waterline was constructed to Lloyds' commercial standards, but to reduce the risk from underwater damage the boiler and turbine compartments were staggered. Although a standard set of cruiser turbines was adopted, destroyer-type boilers gave the rapid acceleration needed for flying operations.

The ships which resulted, the *Colossus* and *Majestic* classes, displaced just over 13,209 tonnes (13,000 tons) but could carry 48 aircraft and had a single catapult. Although only three out of the 16 ordered saw service in the closing stages of the war, they proved their worth post-war, and were undoubtedly one of the most cost-effective small designs ever built. To cure their major drawback, low speed, an improved 'intermediate fleet carrier' design was started in 1943. Power was doubled to add 4-5 knots on a full load displacement of 25,401 tonnes (25,000 tons), and the greater beam allowed better underwater protection. But aircraft capacity was hardly greater than the *Colossus* class, making them less cost-effective. Eight were laid down but only four were completed post-war.

The final British design of World War II was the most powerful to date, but also the most unusual. The 47,754-tonne (47,000-ton) *Malta* class would have been the only Royal Navy carriers to rival the *Midway* class, and were designed along American lines, with sufficient range to operate in the Pacific, a top speed of 33 knots and only splinter-proof armour on the flight deck. However, the closed hangar was retained, limiting the aircraft capacity to 80. Although a fascinating departure from traditional British practice, there is some evidence that the Admiralty was not happy with the design, and they were cancelled in 1945.

By 1943 the gigantic Allied aircraft industry was geared up to meet all demands on it. The Grumman Hellcat proved to be superior even to that remarkable carrier fighter the Zero. The Corsair earned an unfortunate reputation as a 'widow-maker' until the designers realised that the excessive bounce in the undercarriage made it liable to leapfrog over the crash barrier. In desperation it was given to the US Marine Corps, but the fatal deck crashes continued, so it was passed on to the Fleet Air Arm. Fortunately the vice was cured, and the 'bent-winged bastard from Connecticut' became the most successful carrier

strike fighter of the war (though it still always required the highest level of pilot skill). From 1943 onwards the Japanese steadily lost the edge they had enjoyed – even if sufficient carriers and aircraft remained, there were insufficient crews. The depredations of US submarines also reduced the Imperial Japanese Navy's fuel reserves; the submarines' priorities being carriers first, oil tankers second and other warships third.

Japan's Axis partners in Europe had even less luck with their carrier programmes. Wartime shortages in Germany and the need to divert resources to U-boat construction led to the suspension of work on the *Graf Zeppelin* in 1940. The more glaring deficiencies of the design were recognised, and after two more years spent refining the design, work began again in 1942. By this time the Italians were making promising progress on the conversion of two ocean liners, and the catapults were sent to Italy to speed up work. The drubbing the Italian Navy had received at the hands of Cunningham's carriers in 1940-41 opened their eyes at last, and Mussolini's claim that Italy was itself a huge aircraft carrier was seen to be a great mistake. The liner *Roma* was re-engined to boost her speed from 21 to 30 knots (the Italians could never draw a distinction between conversion and new construction, even in the middle of a war), and renamed *Aquila*. She was nearly ready to start her sea trials when Mussolini was overthrown and

Below: The 'Big E', otherwise known as the 'Fighting Lady', the USS *Enterprise* saw action from December 1941 to August 1945.

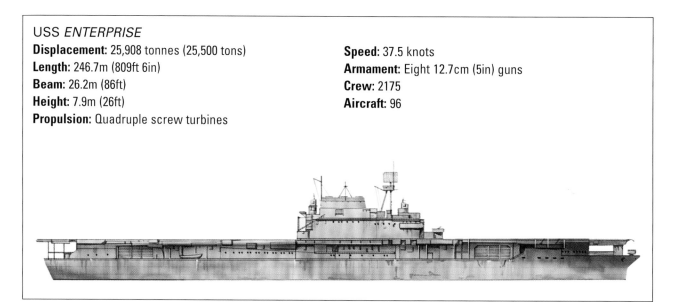

USS *ENTERPRISE*
Displacement: 25,908 tonnes (25,500 tons)
Length: 246.7m (809ft 6in)
Beam: 26.2m (86ft)
Height: 7.9m (26ft)
Propulsion: Quadruple screw turbines

Speed: 37.5 knots
Armament: Eight 12.7cm (5in) guns
Crew: 2175
Aircraft: 96

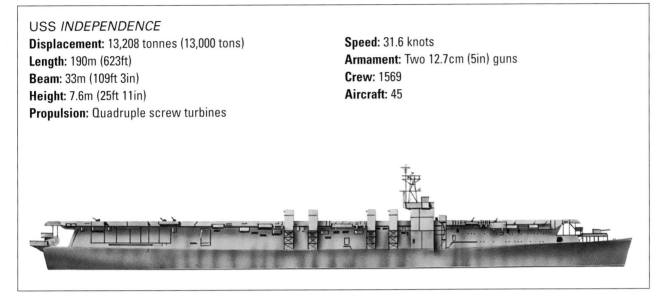

USS *INDEPENDENCE*
Displacement: 13,208 tonnes (13,000 tons)
Length: 190m (623ft)
Beam: 33m (109ft 3in)
Height: 7.6m (25ft 11in)
Propulsion: Quadruple screw turbines
Speed: 31.6 knots
Armament: Two 12.7cm (5in) guns
Crew: 1569
Aircraft: 45

Marshal Badoglio was granted an armistice. She fell into German hands, and inevitably became a target for Allied bombing. After suffering damage she was finally scuttled in 1945. Another conversion, the liner *Augustus*, was to become a CVE and was renamed *Falco* (later changed to *Sparviero*), but she also fell into German hands and was scuttled in 1944.

Only one American carrier saw action in operations off the coast of Northern Europe, the USS *Ranger*, which took part in a strike against German shipping at Bodo in Northern Norway in October 1943. On 3 April 1944 the Home Fleet carriers HMS *Furious* and HMS *Victorious* and four CVEs launched Barracuda dive-bombers against the battleship *Tirpitz*. The defences were taken by surprise, allowing the attackers to hit the *Tirpitz* 14 times. Unfortunately the Fleet Air Arm was restricted to using a 227kg (500lb) bomb, because the RAF insisted that nothing bigger was needed to sink a battleship. (A single hit from a 340kg [750lb] bomb supplied by the US Navy for an earlier attack had very nearly sank the *Tirpitz*, so the Barracuda strike might well have sunk her if they had been allowed to use the heavier bombs.)

A number of devastating strikes were made against German shipping in Norwegian coastal waters, the fleet carriers alone accounting for 101,605 tonnes (100,000 tons), the CVEs supporting them in all operations. Right up to the end of hostilities convoys of war material were run to North Russia, and from February 1944 each one was escorted by CVEs. The constant toll of aircraft contributed to the overall attrition of the *Luftwaffe*, while the CVEs' aircraft took

Above: The light fleet carrier (CVL) USS *Independence* and her sister were both converted on the stocks from light cruisers.

their toll of the U-boats. During this period the venerable Swordfish came into its own as it was sturdy enough to take the stresses of landing on small decks heaving and pitching in the worst weather, while at the same time being powerful enough to carry a search radar and such ordnance as anti-ship rockets. They were used in sweeps against German E-boats (motor torpedo boats), although when flying against a headwind they sometimes had difficulty in keeping up with the target!

In the Pacific the time for defensive measures was also over. By the end of 1943 a Fast Carrier Force, TF 50, was formed under the command of Rear Admiral Charles Pownall. With six fleet carriers and six converted CVLs, it was the most powerful fleet in the world, subdivided into four Task Groups:

TG 50.1 – with the new *Lexington* and new *Yorktown* and CVL *Cowpens* (the Carrier Interceptor Group).
TG 50.2 – with *Enterprise* and CVLs *Belleau Wood* and *Monterey* (the Northern Carrier Group).
TG 50.3 – with *Essex, Bunker Hill* and CL *Independence* (the Southern Carrier Group)
TG 50.4 – with *Saratoga* and CVL *Princeton* (the Relief Carrier Group)

In November 1943 the Carrier Interceptor Group under Rear Admiral Pownall attacked island bases in the Marshalls Group to prevent them from reinforcing

Tarawa and Makin. The Northern Carrier Group under Rear Admiral Radford supported landings on Makin, while the Southern Carrier Group under Rear Admiral Montgomery attacked first Rabaul and then Tarawa. The Relief Carrier Group under Rear Admiral Sherman supported landings in the Solomons and then made a very successful strike against Rabaul. Here at last was carrier warfare as the pre-war theorists had predicted, hitting, retiring and hitting again hundreds of miles away.

A REVERSE PEARL HARBOR

Early in January 1944 TF 50 was renumbered TF 58 and put under the command of Rear Admiral Marc A. Mitscher, formerly captain of the *Hornet* at Midway and also one of the US Navy's most skilled aviators. The reconstituted Fast Carrier Force destroyed all the aircraft defending the Marshalls in a single strike against Kwajalein at the end of the month, with the result that the invasion forces at Kwajalein and Namur suffered not a single bomb-hit. Then it was the turn of Eniwetok, and on 17-18 February TF 58 made the first attack on Japan's 'Gibraltar of the Pacific', the heavily fortified base at Truk in the Caroline Islands. Truk had been the home of the Combined Fleet for nearly two years, and Admiral Nimitz hoped that an attack on such an important target might even tempt the Japanese to intervene with the surface fleet.

In fact the attack turned out to be a sort of Pearl Harbor in reverse. Despite alerts and even a radar warning very few defending aircraft took off in time to cope with the raiders, who sank or damaged nearly 203,210 tonnes (200,000) tons of shipping. In a fierce air battle the Japanese lost over 50 aircraft and another 100 or more were destroyed or damaged on the ground, for the loss of only four Hellcats and nine Avengers. The base was no longer usable, and the Japanese defensive perimeter strategy was in ruins. The sole consolation for the Japanese was a strike by six 'Kates' on the night of 17 February, which slipped through the screen and put a torpedo into the stern of the *Intrepid*. But the *Essex* class were tough ships, and although the carrier's rudder was jammed she was able to return to Majuro Lagoon at 20 knots.

The arrival of HMS *Illustrious* in Ceylon made it possible to stir up yet more trouble for the Japanese. TF 70 was formed with the *Illustrious* and the USS

Right: A technicolour view of the Battle of the Phillipine Sea in June 1944, showing aircraft trying to get back to their carriers.

Saratoga, to operate in the East Indies against Japanese oil and rubber supplies. Under Admiral Sir James Somerville the new Eastern Fleet celebrated its formation with a devastating raid on the oil refinery at Sabang in Sumatra on 19 April. However, the stress of operations showed up weaknesses in the Fleet Air Arm's organisation. For one thing, the air group was very small, and for another, the Barracuda lacked performance. Nor was the vital importance of a quick turn-around of aircraft in the hangar and on the flight deck appreciated at first, and the British had to learn from the battle-hardened veterans of the *Saratoga*. Eventually the Barracudas gave way to the TBF Avengers, and with these the *Illustrious* and *Sara* were able to hit an oil refinery near Surabaya on Java in May.

Despite these losses, the Imperial Japanese Navy still cherished hopes of a decisive battle on its own terms, but the circumstances had altered since 1942. The American carriers were numerous and

Above: A heavy flak barrage put up by the *Enterprise* and her escorts during the Battle of Santa Cruz in October 1942.

were operating much better aircraft and better trained pilots, whereas the Japanese had squandered their skilled pilots with no heed to the future. After the Americans landed on Saipan in the Marianas on 15 June, the Japanese prepared Plan A-Go, to bring about a battle in the vicinity of the Western Caroline Islands. The significance of Saipan was its position as the key to a new 'inner defensive perimeter' which had to be held to keep US bombers out of range of the Home Islands. Plan A-Go relied on the intervention of Japanese land-based aircraft from Guam, Rota and Yap to make up for the shortage of carrier aircraft.

A big reorganisation had been made at the beginning of March, with the Combined Fleet giving way to something closer to the US Navy's task forces.

The First Mobile Fleet was put under the command of Vice Admiral Jisaburo Ozawa, with three carrier divisions:

Carrier Division 1 – *Taiho*, *Shokaku* and *Zuikaku*.
Carrier Division 2 – *Hiyo*, *Junyo* and *Ryujo*.
Carrier Division 3 – *Chitose*, *Chiyoda* and *Zuiho*.

Just how parlous the state of the Japanese Navy had become can be gauged by the fact that Ozawa lacked sufficient top-grade fuel oil to allow his carriers to operate too far afield. Instead his ships were burning the volatile and impure Borneo crude oil. He commanded the largest single force ever entrusted to a Japanese flag-officer, but finding aircrews was a nightmare. The air group for Division 1 had been rebuilt painstakingly from the remnants of an earlier air group destroyed at Rabaul in 1943, and had not joined their carriers until February. Division 2's air group was similarly built on the ruins of an air group

which had been savagely mauled at Rabaul in January 1944, while Division 3 had only been formed at the beginning of February. True, they had the new A6M5 Model 52 Zero, the D4Y 'Judy' dive-bomber, and the B6N 'Jill' torpedo-bomber, but the 'Judy' could not operate from the slow light carriers.

The carriers were sent to Singapore for short refits and were then sent to their forward base at Tawitawi in the Sulu Archipelago off the northeast coast of Borneo. Here they were supposed to exercise their inexperienced aircrews, but this proved virtually impossible. Enemy submarines were active, and on 22 May the *Chitose* was hit by two 'dud' torpedoes, so the First Mobile Fleet was forbidden to go to sea. As there was no airfield at Tawitawi the unfortunate aircrews had very little chance to improve their proficiency.

Below: Flight deck crewmen seen here arming divebombers aboard the USS *Monterey* (CVL.26) in November 1943.

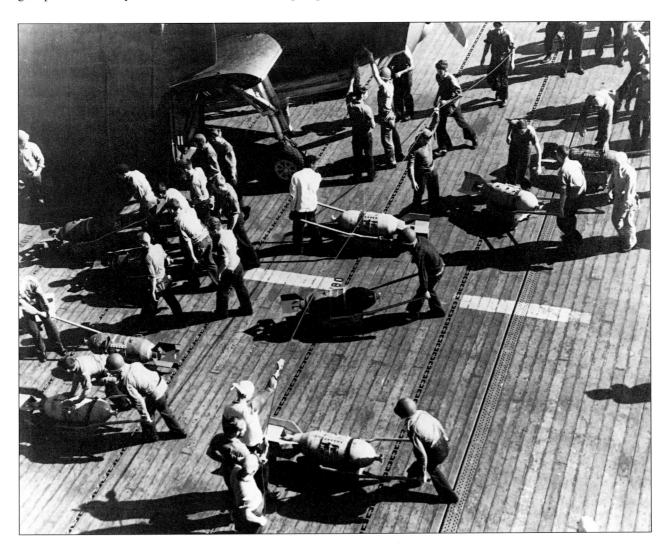

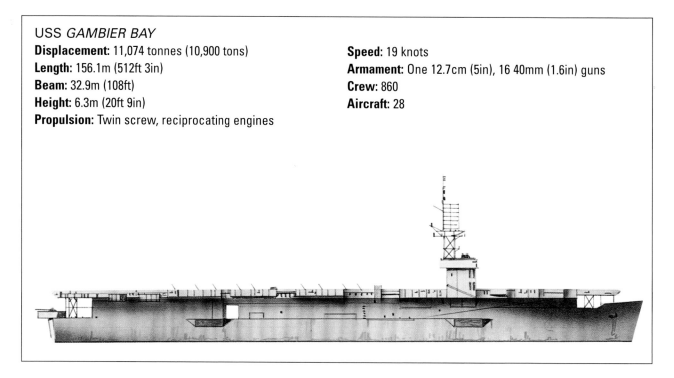

USS *GAMBIER BAY*
Displacement: 11,074 tonnes (10,900 tons)
Length: 156.1m (512ft 3in)
Beam: 32.9m (108ft)
Height: 6.3m (20ft 9in)
Propulsion: Twin screw, reciprocating engines

Speed: 19 knots
Armament: One 12.7cm (5in), 16 40mm (1.6in) guns
Crew: 860
Aircraft: 28

Above: The CVE *Gambier Bay* was one of the 'jeep carriers' which faced the Japanese surface fleet in the Battle of Samar in October 1944.

Ozawa's land-based support was to be provided by Vice Admiral Kakuji Kakuta, commanding the Base Air Force in the Marianas. Because Japanese carrier aircraft were designed without the 'luxuries' of armour protection for the pilot and self-sealing fuel tanks, they could outrange equivalent American aircraft by as much as 338km (210 miles). In theory, therefore, Ozawa could stay out of range and still launch his own strike once the attacks from the Marianas had whittled down the enemy's strength. In fact he intended that his aircraft would fly to Guam, refuel and rearm for a second strike against TF 58 on the way back. He was also banking on the easterly trade winds, which would allow him to launch and recover aircraft while steaming towards the enemy, whereas the American carriers would have to turn into wind every time they operated their aircraft, particularly when recovering them. Plan A-Go also provided for much better reconnaissance than at Midway; Ozawa was determined to avoid the mistake of not locating all US carriers.

TF 58 formed part of the 5th Fleet under Admiral Spruance, whose proverbial caution had been criticised for not securing a bigger victory at Midway, but at the very least he had avoided defeat. Spruance correctly saw his main duty as protection of the Saipan invasion force, and he disposed his four task groups to block any attack by Ozawa against that force. An innovation was to pull the battleships out of the TGs and put them in a Battle Line under Admiral Willis A. Lee. To get to the American carriers the Japanese pilots would have to penetrate a 'picket line' of heavy anti-aircraft fire before encountering each task group CAP and individual ships' anti-aircraft fire.

THE GREAT TURKEY SHOOT

A day after the First Mobile Fleet left Tawitawi on 14 June it was sighted by two enemy submarines, and so 5th Fleet was alerted. Land-based reconnaissance aircraft had overflown TF 58 as early as 11 June, and to forestall the inevitable attacks a massive assault by 208 carrier aircraft was ordered against the Japanese airfields. Kakuta's plans to attack TF 58 were dislocated by almost continuous strikes, and the staging posts on Iwo Jima and Chichi Jima were put out of action, as were Guam and Rota. To make matters much worse Kakuta did not tell Ozawa that he would be facing the American carriers with their air groups virtually intact.

Unaware that he was steaming to destruction, Ozawa ordered his ships into battle formation on the

Right: The USS *Wasp* seen here in June 1942. Although relatively small, she nevertheless managed to embark a large air group.

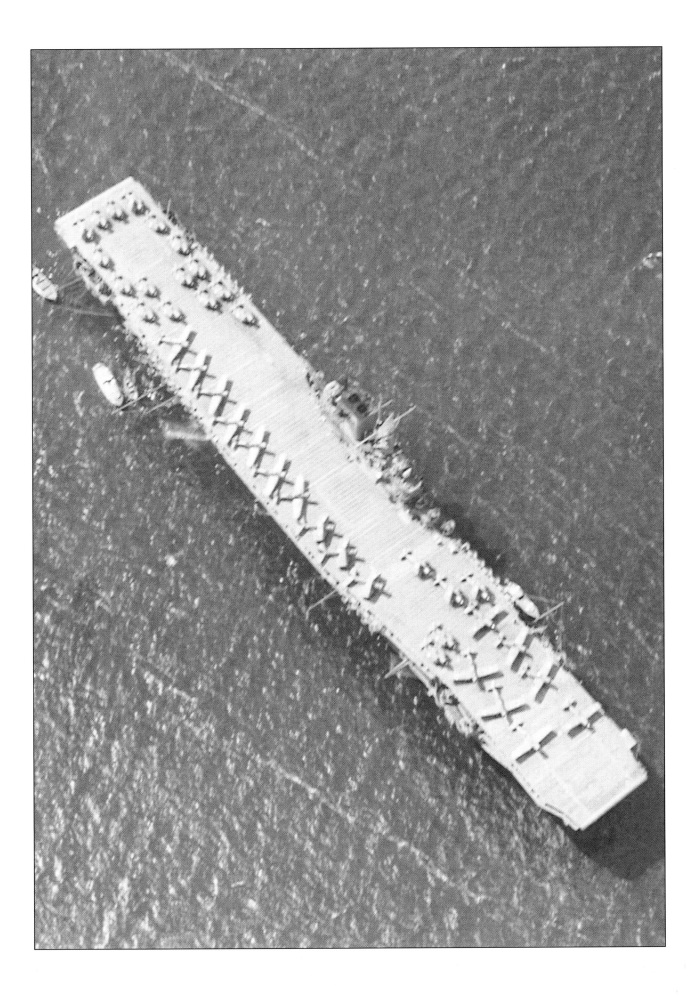

USS *ESSEX*
Displacement: 35,438 tonnes (34,880 tons)
Length: 265.7m (871ft 9in)
Beam: 29.2m (96ft)
Height: 8.3m (27ft 6in)
Propulsion: Quadruple screw turbines
Speed: 32.7 knots
Armament: Twelve 12.7cm (5in) guns
Crew: 2687
Aircraft: 91

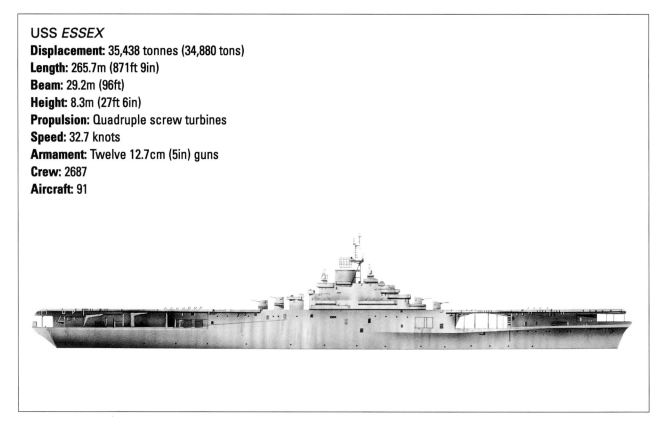

Above: The *Essex* (CV.9) design was probably the best all-round carrier ever built, and they certainly won the Pacific naval war.

Below: The Spanish *Dédaló* was the former CVL, the USS *Cabot*. Two of the original four small funnels were removed.

DÉDALÓ
Displacement: 16,678 tonnes (16,416 tons)
Length: 190m (622ft 4in)
Beam: 22m (73ft)
Height: 8m (26ft)
Propulsion: Quadruple screw turbines
Speed: 30 knots
Armament: Twenty-six 40mm (1.6in) guns
Crew: 1112
Aircraft: 20

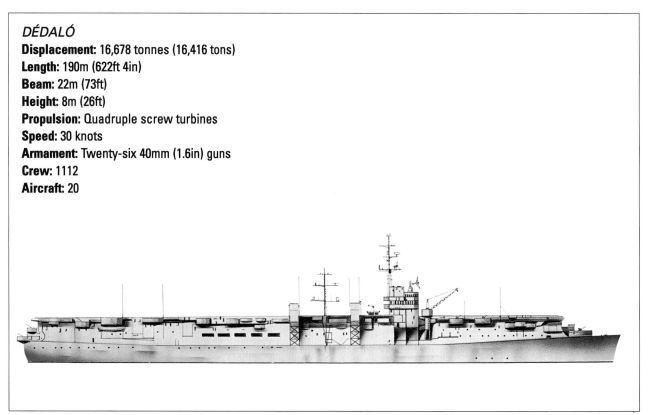

morning of 18 June, with his Van Force under Vice Admiral Kurita commanding the *Chiyoda*, *Chitose* and *Zuiho* 161km (100 miles) ahead of the Main Force, including the remaining carriers in two groups. The first Japanese strike, launched at 0900 hours, was detected on radar by the Battle Line an hour later; it was mauled, losing 32 out of 69 aircraft. A second strike of 110 aircraft shortly afterwards was also shredded by massed gunfire, losing 79 aircraft, with nothing to show for it except a near miss on the USS *Wasp*. Ten minutes after the launch of this second strike disaster struck, when the submarine USS *Albacore* hit the carrier flagship *Taiho* with a single torpedo. The explosion jammed the forward lift and ruptured fuel lines. For six hours it looked as if the carrier's damage control parties would be able to save her, but deadly avgas vapour had filled the ship, and in an attempt to clear the fumes the captain ordered the ship to be turned into wind. At 1530 hours it is

Above: Four *Essex* class: the *Wasp* (CV.18), *Hornet* (CV.12) *Hancock* (CV.19) and *Yorktown* (CV.10) seen here lying at Ulithi Atoll.

believed that a starter-button on an electric pump was pressed. A spark ignited the vapour and a chain-reaction apparently set off the volatile fuel oil, causing the whole ship to erupt in flames. She sank at 1728 hours with the loss of 1650 of her crew.

At 1222 hours another submarine, the *Cavalla*, put four torpedoes into Ozawa's new flagship, the *Shokaku*, setting her ablaze as well. Ozawa still believed that several enemy carriers had been knocked out or sunk, and expected Kakuta's land-based aircraft to launch a massive strike against TF 58. The two fleets drew apart for a while, and Spruance's ships did not sight the Japanese until the following afternoon. He ordered a strike, knowing that at 483km (300 miles) distance his carrier aircraft would not return until after dark, and some might even run out of fuel, but he was gambling on a chance to inflict a really crippling blow on the Japanese. His audacity was rewarded when TF 58's aircraft torpedoed the *Hiyo* and severely damaged the *Junyo*, *Zuikaku* and *Chiyoda*. With the final Japanese losses totalling some 400 carrier aircraft, 100 land aircraft and a number of floatplanes, the jubilant American aircrews dubbed it the 'Great Marianas Turkey Shoot'. It was, effectively, the end of the Japanese Naval Air Force.

It might also have been the end of TF 58 air groups. In ones, twos and threes they made their way back. Admiral Mitscher ordered the carriers to make every effort to close the gap, but it was 2230 hours before the first aircraft were back in the vicinity of the carriers. In a desperate attempt to save as many of his aircrews as possible, Mitscher ordered the mast and

deck lighting to be lit – taking a terrible risk of torpedo attack, but anything to help the exhausted pilots find their carriers. In all, 100 of the 216 aircraft launched were lost, but mercifully most of their crews were rescued – only 20 more aircraft had been lost that day in combat.

A SINISTER DEVELOPMENT

When the Japanese carriers made their last appearance in battle four months later they could only act as decoys to allow the surface fleet to attempt an attack against the US invasion forces in Leyte Gulf in the Philippines. Admiral Halsey pursued Ozawa's decoys, leaving the defence of the invasion fleet to a

Below: An *Essex* class carrier at sea with her deck packed with aircraft. Note the port side lift in the 'down' position.

force of CVEs and destroyers off Samar. In an epic fight the 'jeep carriers' and their escorts held off Japanese battleships and heavy cruisers, losing the CVE *Gambier Bay*, with aircraft making dummy runs against the enemy ships. A sinister development was *kamikaze* suicide attacks against the CVEs, which sank the *St Lô* and damaged the *Suwannee*.

The landings on Okinawa in April 1945 provoked a ferocious onslaught from *kamikaze*s, for in their despair the Japanese could now hope to do no more than postpone the day of reckoning. The *Enterprise*, *Intrepid*, *Bataan* and *Bunker Hill* were all hit, the last named suffering a terrible ordeal. Four British carriers were also involved, HMS *Illustrious*, HMS *Indefatigable*, HMS *Indomitable* and HMS *Victorious*, forming TF 57, but their armoured decks saved them from serious damage. Later a relief carrier, HMS *Formidable*, was hit twice, but like the

Above: With her fires extinguished but listing badly with hundreds of tons of water on board, the USS *Franklin* is taken in tow.

others, she was back in action within a short time. Amazingly, despite heavy casualties, no American or British carrier was sunk by the *kamikaze* suicide attacks.

It took a combination of all arms to bring about the Japanese surrender in August 1945 (not least the dropping of nuclear bombs on the cities of Hiroshima and Nagasaki), but there can be no doubt that the fast carrier task forces played a major role. They and their highly skilled air groups demolished the original 'island chain' of bases, crushed the 'inner perimeter' in turn, and finally destroyed the Imperial Navy's ability to wage offensive war. It had been a long road from Pearl Harbor.

CHAPTER EIGHT

Triumph of the Carrier

World War II proved that the aircraft carrier had become the capital ship of a nation's navy. Today, the massive nuclear-powered aircraft carriers operated by the US Navy represent the apogee of carrier design, development and power projection. At the other end of the scale, smaller navies operate Short Take-Off and Vertical Landing and helicopter carriers, which have proved their worth in conflicts such as the Falklands War.

Although never conceded during the Second World War, the title of 'capital ship' had passed from the battleship to the carrier by the end. The massed anti-aircraft batteries of the battleships had been very useful to protect the task groups, but as weapons-carriers their guns were far outclassed by the bombs and torpedoes of carrier aircraft. Within months of the Japanese surrender battleships were reduced to training or laid up in reserve.

Left: The USS *Carl Vinson* (CVN.70) is one of three *Nimitz* class 90,000-tonne (88,578-ton) nuclear powered carriers built between 1968-82.

Despite this, the years after 1945 saw an acrimonious debate about the future of the carrier. The dropping of the atom bomb led to a frenzy of speculation and wild claims that 'the Bomb' had made all warships obsolete at a stroke. The old *Saratoga* and the damaged CVL *Independence* were among the target-ships at Bikini in 1946, and although the *Sara* sank several hours after the second test, valuable lessons were learned. The cancelled *Essex* class *Reprisal* was used for underwater shock trials, as was the battered *Independence*. Scrapping of older carriers whittled the US Navy's strength down still further, and by the end of 1947 the active force was 20: three

Midway class, eight *Essex* class, two CVLs and seven CVEs. The only unit still to be commissioned was the last *Essex*, the *Oriskany*, which had been suspended to allow improvements to be incorporated. She was finally delivered in 1950.

The only other flourishing carrier force was the Royal Navy, but its wartime programmes were slashed in 1945, leaving three *Illustrious* class (*Formidable* was scrapped because of battle damage), two *Implacable* class and 14 *Colossus* class CVLs (two converted to maintenance carriers), and HMS *Unicorn* as the front-line force. Under construction were two *Eagle* class fleet carriers and four *Hermes* class intermediate fleet carriers.

THE NEW JETS

The French still had the old *Béarn*, serving as an aircraft transport, and the small CVE *Dixmude* on loan from the Royal Navy. In 1946 the British transferred HMS *Colossus*, and she was re-commissioned as the *Arromanches*. The Royal Netherlands Navy was given her sister HMS *Venerable*, renamed *Karel Doorman* to perpetuate the name given to the wartime CVE HMS *Nairana*. Another CVL, HMS *Warrior*, was lent to the Royal Canadian Navy to replace two wartime CVEs, while the Royal Australian Navy acquired HMS *Terrible* in 1948 and renamed her HMAS *Sydney*, followed later by HMAS *Melbourne* (ex-HMS *Majestic*). The Canadians later exchanged HMCS *Warrior* for her sister *Magnificent*, and then bought the upgraded *Powerful* and renamed her HMCS *Bonaventure*. The US Navy also transferred two CVLs to the French Navy in 1950-53, the *Lafayette* (ex-*Langley*) and *Bois Belleau* (ex-*Belleau Wood*).

The most urgent technical question was how to operate jets from carriers? Many experts considered them too dangerous for carrier operations although experiments with Ryan FR-1 Fireballs aboard the USS *Ranger* in 1945 had proved inconclusive. The honour of making the first jet landing on a carrier goes to a British Vampire I fighter, which landed on the CVL HMS *Ocean* on 3 December 1945. Just over seven months later an XFD-1 Phantom took-off from the USS *Franklin D. Roosevelt*. These early jets were sluggish in responding to the throttle and were wildly extravagant on fuel, so propeller-driven types remained in service for many years. The greatest was the Douglas AD-1 Skyraider, the most successful piston-engined attack aircraft of its day.

As early as 1945 the possibility of using carrier aircraft to drop nuclear bombs had been discussed. By coincidence the weight of the 'Fat Man' bomb dropped on Nagasaki, about 4536kg (10,000lbs), was the same as the payload specified for the US Navy's new AJ Savage twin piston-engined carrier bomber. As an interim measure the P2V-2 Neptune could be pressed into service, and it first flew from the *Coral Sea* in April 1948.

The Navy's attempted trespass on the sacred turf of strategic bombing provoked a reaction from the US Air Force not unlike the Billy Mitchell feud in its ferocity. The Navy argued that the dispersion of nuclear 'assets' would reduce the risk of a surprise attack, and asked for funds to research into lighter nuclear weapons for small carrier aircraft. The Air Force, newly independent of Army control, argued that 'big is best', claiming that the B-29 bomber was the best means of delivering the heaviest weapons.

Even the *Midway* class proved a tight squeeze for the Neptune, and so the US Navy drew up plans for a 60,963-tonne (60,000-ton) carrier to be called the USS *United States* (CV.58). She would be the largest warship ever built at that time, 332m (1090ft) long and 40m (130ft) wide at the waterline, and driven by steam turbines at a speed of 33 knots. To facilitate flying operations she would have no island, merely Japanese-style funnels to port and starboard, and a navigating position which could be raised hydraulically when needed. No centreline lifts would be provided, only four deck-edge lifts serving four catapults. The keel of the *United States* was laid at Newport News on 18 April 1949, only 10 days after the Air Force ordered 39 giant six-engined B-36 bombers. The Air Force knew that the $234 million price-tag compared unfavourably with the carrier's budgeted cost of $189 million, and would be challenged by Congress, so it had to be war to the death. The Air Force even went so far as to accuse the Navy of lying, claiming that the true cost of the carrier was $500 million, but other more rational arguments were put forward.

1 – The Navy would duplicate the 'primary' strategic bombing mission of the Air Force.

2 – The Soviet Union was not a sea power, and did not depend on imports of raw materials.

Right: The USS *Ranger* pictured here was one of the original *Forrestal* class 'super carriers' built after the Korean War.

3 – The US Navy and the Royal Navy already had 'overwhelming' superiority over the Soviet Navy.

4 – The carrier-based bomber could only operate within a 1127km (700-mile) radius of land-targets.

If these arguments did not crop up so frequently they would hardly be worth discussing. The first point is illogical, and as history shows, naval aircraft had delivered the first 'strategic' attacks. Points 2 and 3 may have sounded convincing in 1949, but 20 years later at the height of the Cold War they had a hollow ring. Point 4 was demonstrably dishonest: Neptune and Savage bombers had delivered weapons as much as 7725km (4800 miles) away, which implied a radius of 3862km (2400 miles). To be fair to the USAF, the Navy was premature in demanding the diversion of scarce resources at a time when the feasibility of carrier-based nuclear bombing had only just been demonstrated. The argument would inevitably centre on strategic bombing because Congress and many taxpayers were convinced that the next war would be decided by bombing alone. War had not yet become a 'four minute' affair of Intercontinental Ballistic Missiles (ICBMs), but 'conventional' forces like armies and navies were thought to have no future against nuclear attack.

With the benefit of hindsight, the Navy was right to ask for a new carrier but wrong to link it to the strategic bombing role. It paid the price for this and was forced to abandon the *United States* almost as soon as the order was placed. But the defeat did not prevent the Navy from initiating a programme to improve the ability of the *Essex* class to handle modern aircraft. Using the delayed *Oriskany* (CV.34) as the prototype, 22 were earmarked for the SCB 27 modernisation, with stronger decks, longer catapults, more powerful lifts, extra fuel and improved electronics. The only vessels omitted were to be the heavily damaged *Franklin* and *Bunker Hill*.

The airy theorising about the end of conventional warfare was brought to an abrupt end by the outbreak of war in Korea in 1950. Suddenly the United States and its allies were faced with a problem which could not be dealt with by unleashing a nuclear holocaust. To discomfit the air power enthusiasts even more, the carriers were the first reinforcements on the scene when the communist forces of the Democratic People's Republic of Korea crossed the 38th Parallel and drove down the peninsula. The terrain made it difficult to establish airfields quickly, so the carriers' support was vital. For the rest of the war US carriers and those of the Royal Navy, the Royal Canadian Navy and the Royal Australian Navy were constantly on station, supporting land operations and naval bombardments and preventing minelaying. In November 1950 an F9F operating from the USS *Philippine Sea* shot down the first MiG-15 jet fighter, while one of HMS *Ocean*'s piston-engined Sea Furies shot down another in 1952. At the end of April 1951 Skyraiders from the *Princeton* wrecked the Hwaechon reservoir with torpedoes, after USAF B-29s had failed with guided bombs.

Below: The *Forrestal* (CVA.59) design was originally very 'clean' in appearance, but over the years they sprouted antennas and new weapons.

USS *FORRESTAL*
Displacement: 80,516 tonnes (79,248 tons)
Length: 309.4m (1015ft)
Beam: 73.2m (240ft)
Height: 11.3m (37ft)
Propulsion: Quadruple screw turbines
Speed: 33 knots
Armament: Eight 12.7cm (5in) guns
Crew: 2764, 1912 air crew
Aircraft: 90

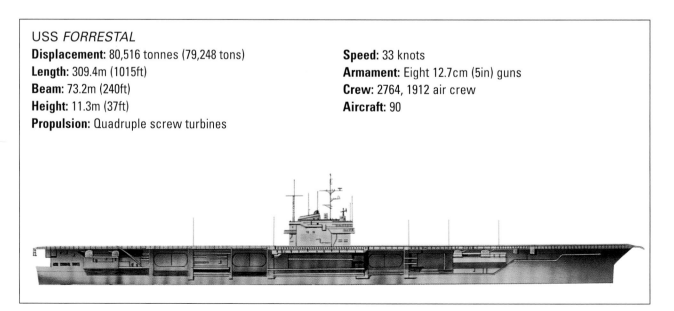

USS *JOHN F. KENNEDY*
Displacement: 81,090 tonnes (79,813 tons)
Length: 324m (1063ft)
Beam: 77m (252ft 7in)
Height: 10.7m (35ft)
Propulsion: Four shaft geared turbines

Speed: 33 knots
Armament: Three Mark 29 launchers, three 20mm CIWS
Crew: 4685
Aircraft: 90

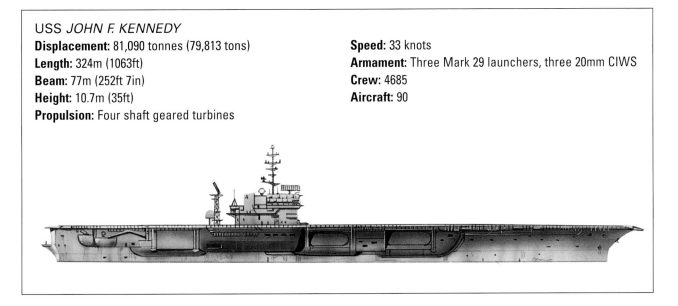

Above: The USS *John F. Kennedy* (CV.67) differed in a number of details from her sisters, but retained the same basic characteristics.

Suddenly the case for the big carrier was back on the agenda, but the technical problems were now manageable, thanks to a number of ideas pursued by the Royal Navy. In 1948 HMS *Warrior* was given a flexible rubber deck, in the hope that aircraft could land without undercarriages or the help of arrester wires. Although the idea worked it was dropped because it would have robbed naval aircraft of flexibility. The next idea was for an angled deck, arising out of a meeting in 1951 to study the growing difficulties of handling heavier aircraft with higher landing speeds. By skewing the the flight deck 10° to port the risk of an aircraft missing an arrester wire and hitting the barrier was reduced. As overshooting pilots only needed to open the throttle and go round for a second attempt, this not only saved pilots but aircrew as well, and reduced the risk of a deck fire.

NEW CATAPULTS

The CVL HMS *Triumph* carried out trials in February 1952, using an angled area painted on the deck, and a few port side obstructions were removed to allow pilots to do 'touch-and-go' landings. Similar trials on board the *Midway* convinced the US Navy, and in September the same year the *Essex* class *Antietam* was taken in hand for conversion. She had an eight-degree angled deck extension, produced by locking the side lift in the 'up' position, and re-aligned arrester wires. In 4000 landings the system was shown to make a major difference to safety.

The next step was to increase the power of catapults, which were no longer capable of launching the latest aircraft. Commander C. C. Mitchell RNVR

produced a design for a catapult using a steam piston driven by the carrier's boilers. For the first time since World War I it was possible to launch aircraft when the carrier was lying at anchor. The first ship with the prototype steam catapult was the maintenance carrier HMS *Perseus*, which went to the United States towards the end of 1951 to demonstrate it. After a series of 140 joint trials the US Navy adopted the system, the first carrier to get it being the USS *Hancock*. The first Royal Navy carrier to get steam catapults was HMS *Ark Royal* in 1955.

The third advance also came from the British, a mirror device to give the pilot precise information about his height and attitude over the flight deck in the final stage of landing. By eliminating the 'batsman' and reducing pilot-error, the mirror landing sight cut the number of deck accidents significantly. In essence, the device allows the pilot to see a row of lights, but only when the aircraft is approaching at the correct height and with wings level. Being non-mechanical it was not subject to increases in landing speeds, and in a greatly refined form it remains in use today, using fresnel lenses.

Before moving on to the era of the super-carrier, it is worth noting that the French Aéronavale had to fight a difficult colonial insurrection in Indo-China. Although on a smaller scale than Korea, it was fought using very much the same tactics. To back up the ex-British *Arromanches*, the CVL *Langley* was acquired from the US Navy in 1951 and renamed *Lafayette*. In fact fighting had been going on since 1946, when Vietminh guerrillas under Ho Chi Minh tried to prevent the French from reoccupying the country. The *Béarn* rushed 4000 troops to Haiphong, and the following year the little CVE *Dixmude* ferried SBD Dauntlesses to help deal with the insurrection. The *Arromanches* and *Lafayette* flew over 1200 sorties to get supplies into the beleaguered fortress at Dien Bien Phu, and although the US Navy transferred a second CVL, the *Belleau Wood*, she arrived at Haiphong a month after the fortress capitulated. In effect this disaster brought an end to the Indo-China War, but brought American intervention closer.

THE SUEZ CRISIS

The Royal Navy was strengthened by the completion of HMS *Eagle* in 1951, but her sister *Ark Royal* was delayed another five years to permit the addition of steam catapults, an angled deck and a side lift. For a variety of reasons, the plans to modernise the wartime fleet carriers had to be cut back. With *Formidable* too badly damaged, *Illustrious* and *Indomitable* worn out, and *Implacable* and *Indefatigable* too costly to modernise, only *Victorious* proved worth saving (the others being relegated to training). Apart from six remaining *Colossus* class, the 22,353-tonne (22,000-ton) *Albion*, *Bulwark* and *Centaur* were completed in 1953-54, but their sister *Hermes* was delayed to allow for improvements.

The seizure of British and French assets along with the nationalisation of the Suez Canal in 1956 triggered an Anglo-French intervention intended to topple the Egyptian president, Colonel Nasser. Whatever else went wrong in that misconceived campaign, the naval air element functioned with surprising efficiency. As late as July 1956 the only operational carrier in the Royal Navy was HMS *Eagle*, yet at the end of October three carriers were available, by bringing HMS *Albion* and HMS *Bulwark* forward from training and refit respectively. Plans to use the CVLs *Ocean* and *Theseus* as troop transports were cancelled and they were converted to helicopter carriers. The US Marine had introduced a technique of 'vertical assault', putting troops ashore by helicopter, but it had not been tested in action. With only two weeks to train, in

Right: The USS *Kitty Hawk* (CVA.63) was one of four improved *Forrestals*, with more powerful steam plant and various other modifications.

Above: The *John F. Kennedy* (CV.67), pictured here replenishing fuel from an auxiliary oiler during the 1991 Gulf War against Iraq.

Below: The *Enterprise* as built, with a distinctive conical structure above the island, and planar radar arrays on its faces.

USS *ENTERPRISE*
Displacement: 91,033 tonnes (89,600 tons)
Length: 335.2m (1100ft)
Beam: 76.8m (252ft)
Height: 10.9m (36ft)
Propulsion: Quadruple screw geared turbines, steam supplied by eight nuclear reactors.

Speed: 32 knots
Armament: Surface-to-air missiles
Crew: 3325, 1891 air group and 71 marines
Aircraft: 99

Above: The USS *Enterprise* (CVN.65) after her service-life extension programme (SLEP), during which her island was altered.

a totally unfamiliar environment, the Royal Marines were now called on to try it for real.

The first carrier strikes against ground targets began on the morning of 1 November 1956, with aircraft from the *Eagle*, *Albion* and *Bulwark* and the French *Arromanches* and *Lafayette*. Although the Egyptian Air Force's MiG-15s gave it superiority on paper, the French and British soon won air superiority. When the helicopter assault was finally sanctioned on 6 November it was a great success,

with 600 Royal Marines flown ashore in 22 Whirlwinds and Sycamores. Despite excessive caution by the Joint Allied Command in exploiting the surprise, in the first hour-and-a-half 415 marines landed, and 20.3 tonnes (20 tons) of supplies, all at the cost of only one helicopter. Whatever else the Suez operations achieved, they showed that the carrier was the most potent weapon for dealing with limited or 'brushfire' wars. They also showed the potential of the helicopter for development.

By now the West had retreated from its belief in nuclear weapons as the only guarantors of world peace. Once the Soviet Union exploded its own nuclear devices some degree of parity had to be accepted, and with that admission came the realisation that 'conventional' forces still had a role. Even while the Korean War was still being fought the US decision against carriers had been reversed, and in July 1952 the keels of two new 60,693-tonne (60,000-ton) carriers were laid. These were the *Forrestal* (CVA.59) and *Saratoga* (CVA.60). The CVA designation was adopted for 'Attack Carrier', and was extended to all the modernised *Essex* and *Midway* classes.

THE *FORRESTAL* CLASS

The *Forrestal* design was a giant step forward in carrier operating techniques. Owing much to earlier studies for the *United States*, it had no centreline lifts, just four large deck-edge lifts (one to port and three to starboard). Although a flush deck was considered, eventually a small island was adopted. A massive sponson on the port side allowed a 101/2 angled deck, with two catapults at the forward end, in addition to two at the forward end of the flight deck. Three other features were reminiscent of British carriers: a smaller number of side openings, defensive guns sited at the corners of the flight deck and an enclosed 'hurricane' bow. The sheer size of the design (317m [1039ft] long overall, 77m [252ft] width across the flight deck) made a number of improvements possible. With 7.62m (25ft) overhead clearance in the hangar, bigger aircraft could be operated, and the combination of deck-edge lifts and four steam catapults made it possible to launch as many as eight aircraft a minute – an important consideration for maintaining a CAP with jet aircraft. Fuel capacity was 70 per cent higher than the *Essex* class, with three times the avgas, and the capacity for one-and-a-half times the number of bombs and rockets.

As the first aircraft carriers ever designed to operate jet aircraft, the *Forrestal* class would also be able to operate the most advanced aircraft, the Banshee, Cougar, Fury and Cutlass, with the Skyray, Demon, Tiger, Crusader and Skyhawk to come. The Skywarrior took over from the unpopular Savage bomber; the 'strategic' role was still regarded as the most important. Eventually the *Essex* class CVAs were assigned two fighter squadrons, one with Demons or Skyrays, and the other with Crusaders, and two or three attack squadrons with Furies,

Right: F-14 Tomcats on the deck of the USS *Enterprise*, a picture that illustrates that no matter how large the carrier space is always at a premium.

USS *NIMITZ*
Displacement: 92,950 tonnes (91,487 tons)
Length: 332.9m (1092ft 2in)
Beam: 40.8m (133ft 10in)
Height: 11.3m (37ft)
Propulsion: Quadruple screw turbines, two water-cooled nuclear reactors

Speed: 30 knots
Armament: Four Vulcan 20mm guns plus three Sparrow SAM launchers
Crew: 5621
Aircraft: 90

Cougars and Skyhawks. The *Midways* and *Forrestals* embarked a sixth squadron of Skywarriors for long-range, all-weather strikes. While deployed in the Western Pacific and the Mediterranean it was normal practice to keep two Skyhawks (light attack) and two Skywarriors fuelled and armed with nuclear bombs as a part of the strategic deterrent. Particularly after the development of ICBMs the seaborne wing of the deterrent was regarded as a valuable insurance against a surprise attack on the United States. The fact that a CVA's position at sea could not be fixed accurately made it an impossible target for an ICBM, whereas sooner or later the position of a land-based ICBM silo could be pin-pointed.

The number of CVAs was fixed at 15 in commission, and it was hoped to build a dozen *Forrestals* to replace the *Essex* class. The force-level of 15 was maintained as far as possible, although sometimes it fell to 14 or increased to 16 because of refit cycles. Two CVAs were maintained in the Sixth Fleet in the Mediterranean and three with the Seventh

Fleet in the Western Pacific. This required that another two carriers be in commission, either coming forward after refit or temporarily in dock for essential maintenance. To keep up the tempo a third *Forrestal* was ordered, the *Ranger* (CVA.61), which was laid down in 1954, followed by the *Independence* (CVA.62) a year later. They were followed by an improved group, the *Kitty Hawk* (CVA.63) and *Constellation* (CVA.64), laid down in 1956-57, the *America* (CVA.66) in 1961 and the much modified *John F. Kennedy* (CVA.67) in 1964.

NUCLEAR POWER

The main differences in the new CVAs were the result of experience with the *Forrestals*. Because the port-side lift was nearly always locked in the 'up' position to extend the forward end of the angled deck, it was decided to position the island further aft. This allowed one of the starboard lifts to be moved forward, while the port lift was repositioned further aft to clear the angled deck area. The forward 12.7cm (5-inch) guns

Above: The *Nimitz* SCB 102 design is in most respects similar to earlier carriers, but only two nuclear reactors drive the ship.

had proved a liability in rough weather, throwing up spray, so they were suppressed in the new ships. Eventually the after 12.7cm (5-inch) guns were also replaced by Sea Sparrow short-range missile systems, while the *Kitty Hawk* was completed with twin launchers aft for Terrier long-range surface-to-air missiles (SAMs).

Instead of building four more steam-powered carriers the important decision was taken to switch to nuclear power. This had certain very clear advantages, including virtually unlimited endurance at high speed, ample reserve steam for the catapults, and the elimination of funnel gases. It also allowed the island to be arranged in a manner which optimised radar performance, and eliminated corrosion of the antennas. The new ship was ordered in Fiscal Year 1958 (FY '58) and was given the honoured name *Enterprise* (CVAN-65). Her keel was laid in February that year and she was launched in September 1960. When she was commissioned at the end of 1961 she was the largest warship ever built, displacing 86,720

tonnes (85,350) tons at full load, 342 m (1123ft) long and 77m (252ft) wide across the flight deck. With the air group embarked, her complement rose to 4600 officers and enlisted personnel. The propulsion plant consisted of eight A2W nuclear reactors, generating steam for four sets of steam turbines, equivalent to a continuous speed of over 30 knots. Configuration was broadly similar to the earlier super-carriers, with no guns. The most conspicuous difference was the compact, square island with its planar radar arrays and a 'turban' top carrying fixed aerials.

The *Enterprise* was also the first carrier equipped with the Naval Tactical Data System (NTDS), a computer-aided device for evaluating and processing data from the ship's own radar, those of her escorts and her aircraft. By using data-link circuits the information could be passed automatically to other ships, allowing a task group to function as a single co-ordinated unit. The 'Big E' had one major drawback: her cost was a staggering $451 million, more than twice the cost of the first *Forrestal* class. Congress was so shocked that it failed to vote funds for another carrier in FY '59 or FY '60. Once again the wisdom of building such large carriers was questioned, but this time it was the Treasury leading the opposition, rather than the Air Force. The US Navy was itself divided on the issue; some senior offices wanted an all-nuclear navy, but others argued that if nuclear propulsion was to cost $100 million extra, it was better to have conventional or 'fossil-fuelled' ships.

THE VIETNAM WAR

Congress compromised by authorising two more *Kitty Hawk* class CVAs in FY '61 and FY '63, after a bitter wrangle, but in FY '67 the decision was reversed with the order for an improved design of nuclear-powered carrier, the *Nimitz* (CVAN-68). Funds for two more followed, for the *Dwight D. Eisenhower* (CVAN-69) in FY '70, and for the *Carl Vinson* (CVAN-70) in FY '74. The logic was inescapable; the *Essex* class had given great service but were wearing out rapidly. Eventually the *Forestal* class would go the same way. Either the carrier was vital to the US Navy, or it had to be phased out altogether and replaced by a more effective means of waging war.

The debate was acrimonious in Congress and the Senate, and continued to be so behind closed doors in the Pentagon. One thing was clear: the carriers offered the only means of carrying the war to the enemy, apart from submarines, but unlike the submarine force, the presence of a carrier task group often proved a deterrent to war. There were growing doubts however about the role of the big carrier in all-out war against the Soviet Navy, with the Russians clearly trying to neutralise the striking power of the carrier by deploying potent anti-ship missiles in surface ships, long-range bombers and submarines.

Meanwhile the US Navy found itself embroiled once more in a war in Asia, this time trying to protect the Republic of South Vietnam from its communist neighbour to the north under Ho Chi Minh, the victor of the struggle against the French. Space does not permit any detailed summary of the sea war off Vietnam, but once again the carriers played a major role. The war dragged on for so long that many innovations were made, but in spite of the advanced aircraft available, the older types gave outstanding service. Epitomising this contradiction, the *Enterprise* was seen with her flight deck crowded with AD Skyhawks, and not a jet-engined aircraft in

Below: The *Dwight D. Eisenhower* (*CVN.69*) was the second *Nimitz* class. The design was so successful that six slightly larger type have been funded.

USS *DWIGHT D. EISENHOWER*
Displacement: 92,950 tonnes (91,487 tons)
Length: 332.9m (1092ft 2in)
Beam: 40.8m (133ft 10in)
Height: 11.3m (37ft)
Propulsion: Quadruple screw turbines, two water-cooled nuclear reactors

Speed: 30 knots
Armament: Four Vulcan 20mm guns plus three Sparrow SAM launchers
Crew: 5621
Aircraft: 90

Above: The *George Washington* (CVN.72) is the second of the *Theodore Roosevelt* (CVN.71) classs, based on the *Nimitz* design.

sight. The *Forrestal* showed how resistant modern carriers are to damage, when a rocket fired accidentally during rearming of aircraft on the flight deck went through 15 decks. Other carriers survived fires and explosion, but returned to duty after short repairs. The Vietnam operations involved the whole gamut of naval air power, from massive air strikes to anti-submarine patrols, ferry operations and amphibious assaults. Not for nothing was it said that the US Navy's carrier exponents owed much to Ho Chi Minh for his help in making the case for carriers.

The Royal Navy found itself in a similar fix in the 1960s, when plans to replace *Eagle* and *Victorious* were drawn up. The design which emerged was designated CVA.01, displaced some 53,851 tonnes (53,000 tons) and was driven by three shaft-geared

steam turbines. Although names were never announced we now know they would have been named *Queen Elizabeth* and *Duke of Edinburgh*. But the RAF was working hard to discredit the carrier concept in order to secure funds for a new supersonic bomber, the TSR.2, and all the fraudulent arguments were marshalled. The hoary old bogey of ICBMs was dragged out to 'prove' that carriers could be knocked out anywhere in the world (no mention of vulnerable airfields). When the Navy raised the question of air cover for naval forces it was assured that shore-based aircraft would always be available.

Above: Powering up into the future is the Rafale M, set to fly from the new French CVN *Charles de Gaulle* in the twenty-first century.

HELICOPTER CARRIERS

The cancellation of CVA.01 and her undeclared sister CVA.02 in 1966 was a severe blow to the Royal Navy with regard to her carrier ambitions, to be compounded by the early demise of HMS *Victorious* after a fire. The surviving carrier, HMS *Ark Royal*, was planned to be taken out of service in 1972. The *Centaur* was to be scrapped, while *Albion* and *Bulwark* were to be converted to 'commando' carriers for the amphibious assault role, operating only helicopters. Although better equipped than her original sisters, HMS *Hermes* was too small to operate a viable air group of modern aircraft, and so she was to be converted to a helicopter carrier for anti-submarine warfare.

A similar compromise had already been made by the US Navy. The US Marine Corps had carried out the first 'vertical assault' trials with the converted CVE *Thetis Bay* (CVAH.1, later LPH.1) in 1955-56, and she had proved so successful that seven *Iwo Jima* (LPH.2) class were built for the purpose. In addition, three unmodernised *Essex* class were converted, *Boxer* (LPH.4), *Princeton* (LPH.5) and *Valley Forge* (LPH.8). Hunting for submarines is equally suited to the talents of the helicopter, and more *Essex* class were converted to Support Carriers (CVS), with a mix of piston-engined S-2F Tracker fixed-wing aircraft and HSS-1 helicopters fitted with dipping sonar.

A number of smaller navies also turned to helicopter carriers. The French Navy had built two

Right: HMS *Ark Royal*, showing her complement of Sea Harrier aircraft and Sea King helicopters. Note the ramp at the bow to facilitate take-offs.

30,482-tonne (30,000-ton) carriers in the 1950s, the *Clemenceau* and *Foch*, as well as a hybrid training cruiser/helicopter carrier, the *Jeanne d'Arc*. The latter had a conventional bow and centreline superstructure forward, and a flight deck aft. Spain acquired the old CVL *Cabot* from the US Navy and renamed her *Dedaló* after a merchant ship converted to operate autogiros in the 1920s.

From the late 1950s the British were working on a revolutionary new aircraft, a Vertical/Short Take-Off and Landing (V/STOL) machine, using vectored thrust from the engine to allow the aircraft to hover in flight. The prototype P.1127 flew in 1960, and it ultimately emerged from exhaustive trials as the Harrier. In 1963 trials were carried out on HMS *Ark Royal*, and thereafter a series of trials was carried out in a wide variety of ships, from helicopter platforms on frigates to the wooden flight deck of the *Dedaló*. V/STOL offered the exciting vista of a bridge between the slow and short-ranged helicopter and the long-ranged but relatively inflexible fixed-wing carrier aircraft, and the Royal Navy ordered an investigation into the new technology.

THE SEA CONTROL SHIP

The drawback to V/STOL at this stage was the inordinate amount of fuel needed to hover or take-off vertically. Even today there are still tasks for which fixed-wing aircraft are inherently more suitable, notably high-speed interception and delivering heavy loads or ordnance on target at maximum range. To the US Navy there was no contest between the available range of carrier aircraft and the relatively primitive V/STOL prototypes. In an attempt to get around this, the US Navy embarked on the design of a Sea Control Ship (SCS), an 'austere' design driven by a single-shaft gas turbine and intended to escort convoys and amphibious groups, with an air group of helicopters and V/STOL aircraft. But after blowing hot and cold for some time it was finally dropped because the naval aviation lobby saw it as a potential distraction from the big carrier programme.

The Royal Navy had little option but to press ahead with its plan to build a helicopter carrier to provide some sort of screen for its surface fleet. Officially the subject of fixed-wing aviation was dead, and although the Harrier continued to be

Right: The small assault carrier USS *Iwo Jima* (LPH.2) acted as a mine countermeasures support ship in the Gulf War in 1991.

Above: The amphibious ships of the *Tarawa* (1-HA-1) class, seen here, are large enough to operate up to 22 AV8B Harrier IIs.

demonstrated in maritime roles no money had yet been invested in a V/STOL aircraft suitable for maritime operations. The workload of navigation made a second seat mandatory, but that pushed up the weight of the aircraft unacceptably, shortening range and reducing bomb-load even more. In fact even the basic terminology was evolving; the V/STOL mode of operating was misleading, because the Harrier functioned more efficiently if it used a rolling take-off, i.e. it was really a Short Take-Off and Vertical Landing (STOVL) aircraft. A vertical launch remained possible for emergencies, but it was very expensive on fuel. When landing back on the carrier, with fuel expended, a 'soft' vertical landing made no difference.

In practice the Royal Navy's surviving fleet carrier HMS *Ark Royal* proved almost indispensable in the numerous minor crises and confrontations which became the pattern of the Cold War in the 1970s. Her tour of duty had to be extended beyond 1972, and it became obvious to all but the government that some sort of replacement was needed. Even when a new design was prepared the political climate was so hostile that it could not even be described as a helicopter carrier – the cumbersome term 'through deck cruiser' had to be used. However, when the details of what was to become HMS *Invincible* were revealed, she had a full-length flight deck and a starboard island. With four gas turbines driving two shafts she would also be the world's largest gas turbine-driven warship.

Meanwhile the British Aerospace designers were refining the Harrier concept, and by the time the Sea Harrier started to take shape on the drawing board, avionics had matured to the point where the second seat and the observer who sat in it could be replaced by a number of pilot-aids to reduce the workload. An engineer officer in HMS *Ark Royal*, noting the way in which heavily laden Phantoms and Buccaneers lost height after being catapulted off, conceived the idea

KIEV
Displacement: 38,608 tonnes (38,000 tons)
Length: 273m (895ft 8in)
Beam: 47.2m (154ft 10in)
Height: 8.2m (27ft)
Propulsion: Quadruple screw turbines

Speed: 32 knots
Armament: Four 7.62cm (3in) guns, plus missiles
Crew: 1700
Aircraft: 36

Above: In 1976 the appearance of the *Kiev* caused consternation in the West, but these hybrids were not successful, and to date three have been scrapped.

Below: The Soviet Navy built the 'helicopter cruisers' *Leningrad* and *Moskva*, but they were never more than a qualified success.

MOSKVA
Displacement: 14,800 tonnes (14,567 tons)
Length: 191m (626ft 8in)
Beam: 34m (111ft 6in)
Height: 7.6m (25ft)
Propulsion: Twin screw turbines

Speed: 30 knots
Armament: One twin SUW-N-1 launcher,
  two twin SA-N-3 missile launchers.
Crew: 850
Aircraft: 18 helicopters

of a 'ski-jump' to reverse the ballistic path. Although of only limited utility for conventional aircraft, it proved ideal for the STOVL aircraft, which used a combination of vertical and forward thrust during take-off. Although initially seen as a safety device, it soon proved to be economical as well, because it allowed a Harrier to save 680kg (1500lb) of fuel on take-off, equivalent to a longer range or a bigger bomb-load. The trials on land were so impressive that HMS *Invincible* was given a ramp on the port side of her flight deck, and HMS *Hermes* was converted back to a 'Harrier carrier' with a much steeper exit-angle to her ski-jump. The ramp is a relatively light structure imposing no severe loads on the hull, and the only other alteration needed was to re-route cable-runs away from the 'hot-spots' created by aircraft warming up on deck.

Although when the *Invincible* was launched in May 1977 she was still officially limited to helicopters, the order for the first FRS.1 Sea Harrier was placed shortly afterwards, and the dimensions of the aircraft had already been taken into account in designing lifts and hangar clearances. In October 1976 an order for a second, *Illustrious*, was announced, and when HMS *Ark Royal* paid off for the last time in December 1978, the third ship, *Indomitable*, was changed to *Ark Royal* to preserve the honoured name.

At the same time, the Soviet Navy finally decided to extend the reach of its naval air arm. In 1968-69 two helicopter carriers were commissioned, the *Leningrad* and *Moskva*, but they were only a qualified success. In 1976 the first of a much bigger type, the Project 1143 hybrid cruiser-carrier *Kiev*, appeared, with a heavy anti-ship missile armament and a nearly full-length angled flight deck. Three more sisters appeared, the 40,642-tonne (40,000-ton) *Minsk*, *Novorosiisk* and the heavily modified *Admiral Gorshkov*, creating consternation in the West. In the early 1980s evidence appeared showing a much bigger 66,043-tonne (65,000-ton) carrier under construction at Nikolaiev in the Black Sea, the Project 1143.5 *Admiral Kuznetsov*. Even more sinister was the news of a 71,124-tonne (70,000-ton) nuclear-powered carrier, the Ulyanovsk.

One of the major props of the argument against large carriers had been the fact that the Soviet Navy didn't have any, so why did anyone else need them?

Left: The *Kiev* looked good, but was nevertheless only a qualified success being neither wholly a cruiser nor an aircraft carrier.

The evidence of Soviet intentions was sufficient to silence these critics, and big carriers were back in favour in Washington. In the mid-1970s the strategic role was finally reduced, and the designation CV or CVN was adopted to signal the more general-purpose air groups to be embarked. In 1981 the first of six improved *Nimitz* type CVNs was laid down, the *Theodore Roosevelt* (CVN-71), for commissioning in 1986. Also a number of Service Life Extension Program (SLEP) modernisations were planned for the CVs and the *Enterprise*. At the time of writing (1999) all six of the new CVNs are in service, funds are approved for CVN-77, and radical changes for the next class, designated CVX, are in hand. The SLEPs won valuable time for the replacement programme, but most of the CVs have reached the end of their lives.

THE 1991 GULF WAR

It might be thought that these developments marked the end of Air Force efforts to undermine the carrier as an effective weapon, but this is not so. During the 1980s the Pentagon became exasperated with the Navy's management of its aircraft procurement programme. The expensive A-12 'stealth' carrier aircraft was cancelled, forcing the Navy to fund a drastic upgrading of the F/A-18 Hornet combined fighter/attack aircraft, a programme which only began to yield results at the end of 1998, when the prototypes began flight-testing. In all, some $7 billion was spent without a single new aircraft joining the Fleet.

When Saddam Hussein's Iraqi army invaded Kuwait in August 1990 the carriers were, as usual, first on the scene, and it is clear that they would have been the only way of stopping an Iraqi drive into Saudi Arabia. However, Saddam's generalship was not up to such sophisticated thinking, and the US government had time to put together a coalition of allies working under a United Nations mandate to expel the Iraqis from Kuwait. In the Gulf War which finally erupted into its short but violent life early in 1991, carrier strikes accounted for 35 per cent of the coalition's air attacks on Iraq. This interesting statistic was played down by the US Air Force's publicity machine in Washington. When mobile launchers of 'Scud' short-range ballistic missiles proved dangerous the Air Force found it could not divert forces from its Air Tasking Order (ATO), a giant air-traffic management plan, and Navy aircraft were given the 'non-strategic' mission of 'Scud-busting'. To make matters worse, once the Iraqi Army had surrendered (to ground forces) the Air Force publicity

machine turned on the Navy. The carriers were apparently capable only of maintaining a CAP over themselves, a canard which ignored the critical role of the carrier battle groups in guarding against any intervention by the Iranian air force or the Iraqi air squadrons which had taken refuge in Iran at the outbreak of the war.

Another more devastating blow was sustained by the US Navy in 1991. Although, strictly speaking, nothing whatever to do with naval aviation in a military sense, the Tailhook scandal tarnished the lustre of the aviators at a dangerous moment. An annual event, the Tailhook Convention was intended to be an opportunity for the naval aviation 'community', aircrew, senior officers and even representatives of the aircraft industry to discuss matters of mutual interest. But over the years the entertainment aspect of Tailhook had come to dominate any serious professional discussions. The 1991 convention in Las Vegas 'got out of hand', and several disturbing cases of sexual impropriety were reported, including the barracking of female pilots by their male counterparts during an exchange of views with the Chief of Naval Operations (CNO) and his Head of Naval Aviation. After the bruising encounter with the Air Force over the Gulf War, Tailhook resulted in disciplinary action against officers and even the premature retirement of the CNO and the chief naval aviator. As years go, 1991 was not a good vintage for the US naval aviators.

In the same time span the Soviet Union has collapsed, taking with it the Navy's ambition to challenge the US Navy as a major sea power. The first three *Kiev*s were sold for scrapping in 1993, and negotiations are in hand with the Indian Navy to transfer the *Admiral Gorshkov*. The *Admiral Kuznetsov* is still carrying out extended trials with the Northern Fleet, but her sister *Varyag* was never completed, and the independent government of the Republic of the Ukraine has been trying to find a buyer for the hulk. The *Ulyanovsk* was also a victim of the split between Russia and the Ukraine, and after work was stopped in 1991 the hull was broken up on the slipway.

THE *INVINCIBLES*

For some years there were rumours of the *Varyag* going to the People's Republic of China, but turning the largely cannibalised hull into a seagoing warship would have been ruinously expensive, and the Chinese People's Liberation Army-Navy lost interest.

For the British, sniping against even the limited capacity of the *Invincible* class continued in the

1980s. In 1981, when the Royal Australian Navy was seeking a replacement for the old CVL HMAS *Melbourne*, the UK Ministry of Defence promptly offered to sell HMS *Invincible*. Her new name had even been selected, HMAS *Australia*, when the news came through of Argentina's invasion of the Falkland Islands in April 1982. The Royal Navy immediately despatched a task force headed by HMS *Hermes* and accompanied by the *Invincible*, with every available FRS.1 Sea Harrier. The Sea Harrier acquitted itself brilliantly, using the AIM-9L Sidewinder missile to deadly effect. Just as the US Navy owed a debt to Ho Chi Minh, the Fleet Air Arm now had General Galtieri to thank for his timely support. Nothing more was heard about the sale of HMS *Invincible*, and her sister *Illustrious* was rushed to completion in time to relieve her at the end of hostilities in June 1982. The *Ark Royal* was delayed because some equipment had been diverted to her sister to speed completion, and she

Above: HMS *Hermes* seen here laid up before being sold to the Indian Navy as INS *Viraat* in 1983. She will serve until 2010.

emerged three years later with a more pronounced 12-degree ski-jump and other improvements. Since then, both *Invincible* and *Illustrious* have been modernised, and in 1998 *Illustrious* lost her twin Sea Dart missile-launcher and magazine to make room for additional deck-space for RAF GR.7 Harrier ground-attack aircraft. The same 'nose job' is to be given to her sisters when they are docked for future modernisations.

Since 1982 the *Invincibles* have seen strenuous service, and at the beginning of 1998 *Invincible* herself was involved in a stand-off between the Iraqi dictator Saddam Hussein and the US and Britain. The FRS.1 Sea Harrier has been replaced by the F/A.2 upgraded variant, with Blue Vixen radar replacing the

Blue Fox, and AIM-120 AMRAAM air-to-air missiles in place of the AIM-9L Sidewinders. As more Sea Harriers have been procured the size of the air group has risen steadily from the original five to as many as 15, and in the last Gulf crisis she temporarily operated 24 aircraft, including Sea King helicopters. For the foreseeable future six RAF GR.7 Harriers will be more or less permanently embarked, a remarkable transition for what were at one time considered ships of very limited capability.

More recently, plans have been maturing to replace the *Invincible* class, and in July 1998 after a Strategic Defence Review was carried out by the incoming Labour government, it was announced that two new carriers would be built in the next century. The design is still evolving, but it seems certain that they will displace about 50,802 tonnes (50,000 tons) and will be driven by a new Integrated Fully Electric Propulsion (IFEP) system, using gas turbines to drive turbo-generators. The advantage of IFEP will be a single power-source for auxiliary power as well as main drive, with no noisy gearboxes and no need for heavy reversing gear or controllable-pitch propellers. It is hoped that the Future Carriers or CV(F)s will operate the STOVL variant of the American Joint Strike Fighter, but alternative plans have been canvassed for a naval version of the Typhoon Eurofighter. This is not popular with the Royal Navy, which has no wish to see the overall size of CV(F) rise, with the added weight (and expense) of catapults and arrester wires.

In the meantime, the Royal Navy has remedied a long-felt need for a dedicated amphibious carrier to work with the Royal Marines, replacing the long-gone *Albion* and *Bulwark*. Although in theory the *Invincible* class could embark a 600-strong marine commando force, in practice it proved very difficult. For one thing, it meant sending the entire air group ashore, and for another, it entailed severe crowding and discomfort for the marines, in ships not tailored for an additional 600 people's catering and washing needs. In 1992 a new LPH was ordered, and she was commissioned in 1998 as HMS *Ocean*. The hullform of the *Invincible* was adapted, becoming slightly beamier, diesels replaced the gas turbines (producing a modest 17 knots) and commercial standards were adopted for the hull. This combination had the supreme virtue of cheapness, at a

Left: HMS *Hermes* was the flagship of the Royal Navy's Task Force sent to recapture the Falkland Islands in 1982.

GIUSEPPE GARIBALDI
Displacement: 14,072 tonnes (13,850 tons)
Length: 180m (591ft 2in)
Beam: 30.4m (99ft 9in)
Height: 6.7m (22ft)
Propulsion: Two shafts, four turbines
Speed: 20 knots

Armament: Four SSM, two SAM launchers, six 40mm guns
Crew: 825
Aircraft: 16

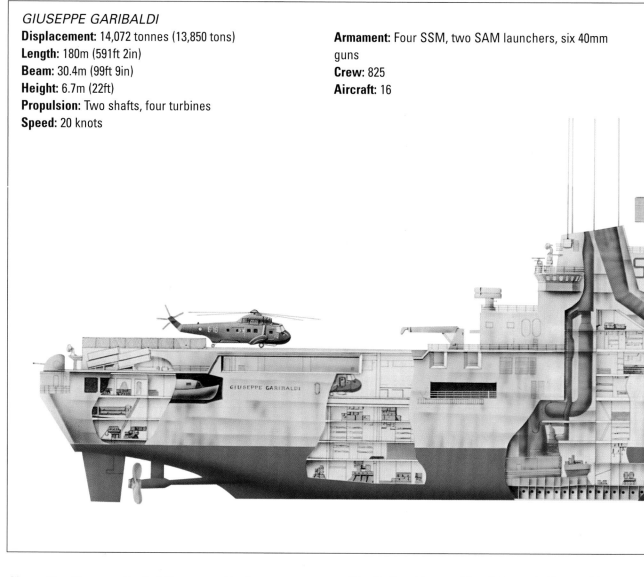

Above: The *Giuseppe Garibaldi* is powered by four Fiat/GELM2500 gas turbines, and also carries a powerful defensive armament.

time when the naval budget was under severe pressure, and to date she has proved very successful.

STOVL has allowed smaller navies to get back into the carrier business. The Spanish Navy bought the design of the defunct Sea Control Ship off the US Navy and since 1988 has operated the 16,968-tonne (16,700-ton) *Principe de Austrias* with conspicuous success. She operates ex-US Marine Corps AV-8A Matador variants of the Harrier, and is currently re-equipping with the AV-8B Harrier Plus. The builders of the *Principe de Austrias*, Empresa Nacional Bazán, adapted the design for the Royal Thai Navy, replacing the single-shaft gas turbine with twin-shaft diesels. She is in service as HTMS *Chakkrinareubet*.

The Italian Navy suffered from similar problems to the Royal Navy, since Mussolini had enacted legislation in the early 1920s giving the Air Force sole responsibility for aviation. But, unlike the British experience, 40 years after the ignominious death of Mussolini and the eradication of his fascist state, that legislation was still being used by the Italian Air Force to stifle any plans by the Navy to acquire STOVL aircraft. The 13,209-tonne (13,000-ton) support carrier *Giuseppe Garibaldi* came into service in 1985, but it took another seven years to rescind the law to allow the Navy to buy the Harrier Plus from the United States. The experience of the Royal Navy in the Falklands War in 1982 carried considerable weight in the debate.

Right: The French *Jeanne d'Arc* was designed as a hybrid training ship and helicopter carrier, but has never operated combat helicopters.

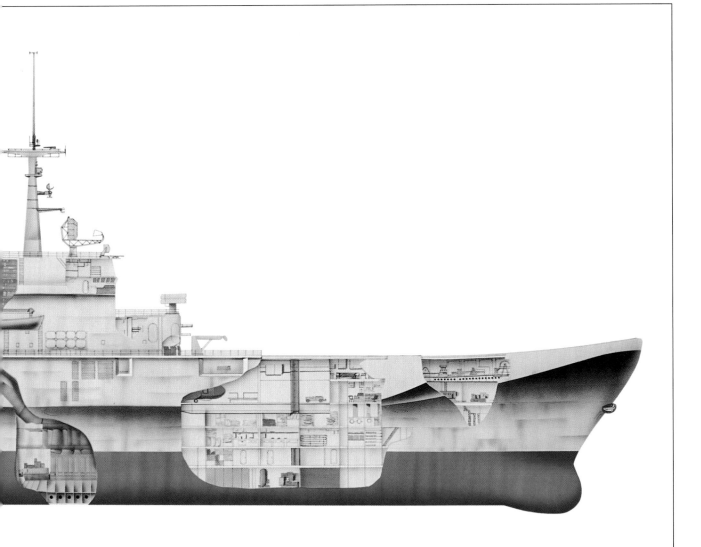

JEANNE D'ARC
Displacement: 13,208 tonnes (13,000 tons)
Length: 180m (590ft 6in)
Beam: 25.9m (85ft)
Height: 6.2m (20ft 4in)
Propulsion: Twin screw turbines
Speed: 26.5 knots

Armament: Four 10cm (3.9in) guns
Crew: 627, plus 198 cadets
Aircraft: Eight

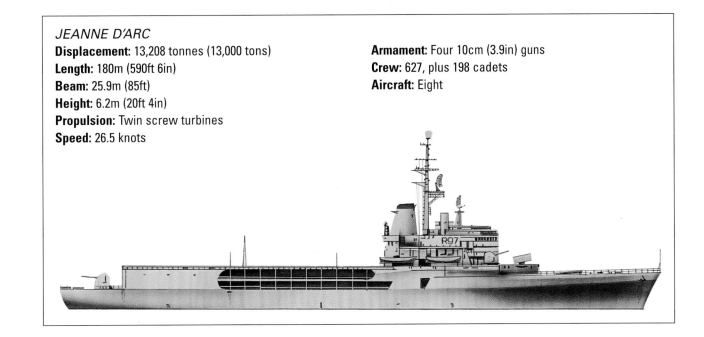

Left: The Italian Navy's 12,000-tonne (11,810-ton) STOVL/helicopter carrier *Giuseppe Garibaldi* pictured here under construction at Monfalcone.

Above: Launch of the Spanish Navy's carrier *Principe de Asturias* at Ferrol in May 1982, a vessel that put Spain back in the carrier buisiness.

The Indian Navy also took the STOVL route, equipping the old CVL *Vikrant* with FRS.1 Sea Harriers, and the *Viraat* (ex-HMS *Hermes*). Plans to build a new class of indigenous carrier, the first to be ready in 1997, were abandoned, and at the end of 1998 a purchase of the Russian *Admiral Gorshkov* was openly discussed, but no confirmation has been announced. Plans for a French design and then an Italian one had previously been dropped; a severe shortage of hard currency seems to be a major cause of the delays. If the Russian purchase goes through it is possible that the Indian Navy may fly MiG-29K and Su-33 aircraft off her decks.

Never to be outdone, the French Navy decided in 1980 that it needed a pair of nuclear-powered carriers to replace the *Clemenceau* and *Foch* in the early 1990s. Hull dimensions were to be virtually the same as the existing carriers to allow the CVNs to be built

in dock at Brest, resulting in a full load displacement of less than 40,642 tonnes (40,000 tons). Using a pair of reactors designed originally for submarines led to the surprisingly modest speed of 27 knots. Shortage of funds delayed the programme, and the keel of the first was not laid until 1989, with the name *Charles de Gaulle* bestowed after the death of the former President. Since then the argument has been mainly focused on the procurement of suitable aircraft. The Aéronavale wanted to accept an American offer to lease F/A-18 Hornets, but political considerations forced it to accept the expensive Rafale-M from Dassault Aviation. Funding problems continued to plague the building programme, and although launched in 1994 the new CVN was not ready to start sea trials until the end of 1998. Early in 1999, during these trials, she suffered an electrical fire and was towed back to Brest.

Above: Spanish Navy Harrier II Plus STOVL aircraft pictured here on the flight deck of the *Principe de Asturias*. The Harrier can operate without long landing decks, catapults and arrestor gear, and is thus perfect for V/STOL aircraft carriers. That said, the small size of the ship means few can be carried.

Left: The Italian *Giuseppe Garibaldi* leads the Spanish *Principe de Asturias* in Exercise 'Dragon Hammer' in May 1992. The latter vessel is based on the design of the US Navy's Sea Control Ship (which was never built), with the addition of a ski jump.

Although the official policy of building a second CVN is still in place, privately it is agreed that such a ship cannot be funded. Yet, with the *Clemenceau* already gone and the *Foch* to be withdrawn from service shortly, a second carrier is essential. At the Euronaval exhibition in Paris in October 1998 a startling solution was proposed: to build a third CV(F) at Brest, in effect a joint Anglo-French carrier programme. This may seem far-fetched, but the French Navy is so short of funds that it may prove to be the only way to fund a second carrier. As a solution it leaves many questions unanswered, particularly what would happen if the Royal Navy's programme were to be axed, or what aircraft will fly from the French CV? A tie-up with the French might seem superficially attractive for the British, but it would limit their options for CV(F)'s equipment, as the French would inevitably demand that French equipment such as radar is made common to all three ships.

Although few navies can afford aircraft carriers, there is a growing vogue for what have been termed 'air-capable' ships. These are warships equipped to operate helicopters and even STOVL aircraft on a temporary ad hoc basis. Notably these include amphibious ships, following the example set by the US Navy and the Royal Navy. In the US the *Iwo Jima* (LPH.2) class helicopter carriers were often used to operate AV-8A or AV-8B Harriers to provide the Marines with ground support. This process continued when much bigger assault ships, the *Tarawa* (LHA.1) and *Wasp* (LHD.1) classes were introduced. These huge multi-purpose ships can operate up to 22 STOVL aircraft from their full-length flight decks. The 20,321-tonne (20,000-ton) LPH HMS *Ocean* is not intended to operate Sea Harriers but could operate them in an emergency.

HALF MEASURES

Large amphibious ships such as dock landing ships (LPDs) are routinely fitted with large flight decks to accommodate medium-lift helicopters, and these can also be used as temporary decks by STOVL aircraft needing to refuel and even rearm. The Italian Navy operates three LPDs designed with flush decks and starboard islands, and when the Japanese Maritime Self Defence Force ordered a similar type of ship, the *Osumi*, the Opposition in the Diet accused the government of fostering 'militarism' in the form of an aircraft carrier! The truth is that both STOVL aircraft and helicopters bring so much extra flexibility to naval operations that even such hybrid ships are better than nothing. All navies realise that to fight without any sort of air cover can invite potentially crippling losses, especially when the opposition possess aircraft armed with even crude anti-ship missiles, as was the case in the 1982 Falklands War, when Exocet missiles took their toll of British ships.

Right: The Spanish Navy's *Principe de Asturias* has an unusual overhanging aircraft lift at the rear end of its 175.3m- (575.1ft-) long flight deck. Note the ski ramp arrangement at the bow.

Epilogue

Above: Early experiments with Harriers led the Spanish Navy to operate AV-8A Harriers from the old CVL *Dédalo*.

The aircraft carrier has come a long way in the twentieth century, from an absurdly primitive state before World War I to the status of new capital ship at the end of the Second. Since then it has survived equally serious attempts to destroy it, mostly from its political enemies. Its critics point to its alleged vulnerability, but it has proved more durable than many land bases on foreign soil. In the post-Cold War period of international instability governments are beginning to realise that a carrier, like its escorts, is sovereign territory, and no negotiations are needed when it arrives off the coast of a foreign state. It can be close, as a friendly ally, or it can be over the horizon, ready to strike, but it is always the first to arrive at a trouble-spot.

New technology may make future carriers even more effective, but in essence the ship with the big deck will remain as part of the order of battle. Big air groups are terrifyingly effective weapons of war today, just as they were in the Pacific during World War II. Now, as then, the aircraft carrier brings together the flexibility of maritime operations and the sheer power of combat aircraft to produce an awesome combination.

The US Navy's carrier battle group represents the apogee of the aircraft carrier as the most powerful naval vessel currently in service. Containing one or two carriers, each capable of deploying an air wing, they represent a massive capacity for force projection. But of course carriers are not invulnerable, and they require substantial assets to protect them from both air and submarine attack. This cover comprises guided-missile cruisers, guided-missile destroyers, anti-submarine warfare destroyers, anti-submarine warfare frigates and even one or two nuclear submarines. And yet each carrier battle group has the potential to sink an entire fleet of enemy vessels – testament to its massive power.

Ships Fitted to Operate Aircraft and Seaplanes in World War I

ROYAL NAVY

Converted cruiser: *Hermes*

Purpose-built
seaplane carrier: *Ark Royal*

Capital ships: *Ajax, Australia, Barham, Bellerophon, Benbow, Canada, Collingwood, Conqueror, Courageous, Emperor of India, Erin, Glorious, Indomitable, Inflexible, Iron Duke, King George V, Lion, Malaya, New Zealand, Orion, Princess Royal, Queen Elizabeth, Ramillies, Renown, Repulse, Revenge, Royal Oak, Royal Sovereign, Tiger, Valiant, Warspite*

Cruisers: *Aurora, Birkenhead, Caledon, Calliope, Carlisle, Caroline, Cassandra, Chatham, Comus, Constance, Cordelia, Coventry, Dauntless, Delhi, Dragon, Dublin, Dunedin, Galatea, Inconstant, Melbourne, Penelope, Phaeton, Royalist, Southampton, Sydney, Undaunted, Weymouth, Yarmouth*

Seaplane carriers: *Anne, Ben-my-Chree, Campania, Empress, Engadine, Manxman, Nairana, Pegasus, Raven II, Riviera, Vindex*

Aircraft carriers: *Argus, Furious, Vindictive Eagle* (building), *Hermes* (building)

Note: Many minor war vessels were also fitted to operate seaplanes

US NAVY

Capital ship: *Texas* (BB35)

Cruisers: *Huntington* (CA5), *Seattle* (CA11), *North Carolina* (CA12)

ITALY

Seaplane transports: *Elba, Europa*

JAPAN

Seaplane carrier: *Wakamiya*

Aircraft carrier: *Hosho* (building)

RUSSIA

Seaplane carriers: *Orlitsa, Imperator Alexander I, Imperator Nikolai* [1], *Regele Carol* [1], *Dakia* [1], *Imperator Trajan* [1], *Rumniya*

Note
[1] lent by Rumanian Government 1916

Aircraft Carriers Completed 1919-1941

US NAVY

USS *Langley* (CV1)	Commissioned 1922
USS *Lexington* (CV2)	Commissioned 1927
USS *Saratoga* (CV3)	Commissioned 1927
USS *Ranger* (CV4)	Commissioned 1933
USS *Yorktown* (CV5)	Commissioned 1936
USS *Enterprise* (CV6)	Commissioned 1938
USS *Wasp* (CV7)	Commissioned 1941
USS *Hornet* (CV8)	Commissioned 1941

JAPAN

Hosho	Commissioned 1922
Akagi	Commissioned 1927
Kaga	Commissioned 1928
Ryujo	Commissioned 1933
Soryu	Commissioned 1937
Hiryu	Commissioned 1939
Shoho	Commissioned 1940
Shokaku	Commissioned 1941
Zuikaku	Commissioned 1941 (converted from auxiliary 1940 + sister *Zuiho* still converting)

ROYAL NAVY

HMS *Furious*	Commissioned 1917
HMS *Argus*	Commissioned 1918
HMS *Eagle*	Commissioned 1923
HMS *Hermes*	Commissioned 1925
HMS *Glorious*	Commissioned 1930
HMS *Courageous*	Commissioned 1930
HMS *Ark Royal*	Commissioned 1938
HMS *Illustrious*	Commissioned 1940
+ 5 *Illustrious* class	Under construction or approved

FRANCE

Béarn	
2 *Joffre* class	Stopped 1940

GERMANY

1 *Graf Zeppelin* class	Under construction
1 *Graf Zeppelin* class	Projected

APPENDIX 3

Aircraft Carrier Programmes in World War II

US NAVY

Essex class: *Essex* (CV9), *Yorktown*[1] (CV10), *Intrepid* (CV11), *Hornet*[1] (CV12), *Franklin* (CV13), *Ticonderoga* (CV14), *Randolph* (CV15), *Lexington*[1] (CV16), *Bunker Hill* (CV17), *Wasp*[1] (CV18), *Hancock* (CV19), *Bennington* (CV20), *Boxer* (CV21), *Bon Homme Richard* (CV31), *Leyte* (CV32), *Kearsarge* (CV-33), *Oriskany* (CV34), *Reprisal*[2] (CV35), *Antietam* (CV36), *Princeton*[1] (CV37), *Shangri-la* (CV38), *Lake Champlain* (CV39), *Tarawa* (CV40), *Valley Forge* (CV45), *Philippine Sea*[2] (CV47), CV50-55[2]

Independence class: *Independence* (CVL22), *Princeton* (CVL23), *Belleau Wood* (CVL24), *Cowpens* (CVL25), *Monterey* (CVL26), *Langley* (CVL27), *Cabot* (CVL28), *Bataan* (CVL29), *San Jacinto* (CVL30)

Saipan class: *Saipan* (CVL48), *Wright* (CVL49)

Midway class: *Midway* (CVB41), *Franklin D Roosevelt* (CVB42), *Coral Sea* (CVB43), CVB44[2], CVB56-57[2], *Long Island* (CVE1), *Charger* (CVE30)

Bogue class: *Bogue* (CVE9), *Card* (CVE11), *Copahee* (CVE12), *Core* (CVE13), *Nassau* (CVE16), *Altamaha* (CVE18), *Barnes* (CVE20), *Block Island* (CVE21), *Breton* (CVE23), *Croatan* (CVE25), *Prince William* (CVE31)

Sangamon class: *Sangamon* (CVE26), *Suwanee* (CVE27), *Chenango* (CVE28), *Santee* (CVE29)

Casablanca class: *Casablanca* (CVE55), *Liscombe Bay* (CVE56), *Anzio* (CVE57), *Corregidor* (CVE58), *Mission Bay* (CVE59), *Guadalcanal* (CVE60), *Manila Bay* (CVE61), *Natoma Bay* (CVE62), *St Lô* (ex-*Midway*) (CVE63), *Tripoli* (CVE64), *Wake Island* (CVE65), *White Plains* (CVE66), *Solomons* (CVE67), *Kalinin Bay* (CVE68), *Kasaan Bay* (CVE69), *Fanshaw Bay* (CVE70), *Kitkun Bay* (CVE71), *Tulagi* (CVE72), *Gambier Bay* (CVE73), *Nehenta Bay* (CVE74), *Hoggatt Bay* (CVE75), *Kadashan Bay* (CVE76), *Marcus Island* (CVE77), *Savo Island* (CVE78), *Ommaney Bay* (CVE79), *Petrof Bay* (CVE80),

Rudyerd Bay (CVE81),
Saginaw Bay (CVE82),
Sargent Bay (CVE83),
Shamrock Bay (CVE84),
Shipley Bay (CVE85),
Sitkoh Bay (CVE86),
Steamer Bay (CVE87),
Cape Esperance (CVE88),
Takanis Bay (CVE89),
Thetis Bay (CVE90),
Makassar Strait (CVE91),
Windham Bay (CVE92),
Makin Island (CVE93),
Lunga Point (CVE94),
Bismarck Sea (CVE95),
Salamaua (CVE96),
Hollandia (CVE97),
Kwajalein (CVE98),
Admiralty Islands (CVE99),
Bougainville (CVE100),
Matanikau (CVE101), *Attu*
(CVE102), *Roi* (CVE103),
Munda (CVE104)

Commencement Bay class:
Commencement Bay
(CVE105), *Block Island*[1]
(CVE106), *Gilbert Islands*
(CVE107), *Kula Gulf*
(CVE108), *Cape Gloucester*
(CVE 109), *Salerno Bay*
(CVE110), *Vella Gulf*
(CVE111), *Siboney*
(CVE112), *Puget Sound*
(CVE113), *Rendova*
(CVE114), *Bairoko*
(CVE115), *Badoeng Strait*
(CVE116), *Saidor*
(CVE117), *Sicily* (CVE118),
Point Cruz (CVE119),
Mindoro (CVE120), *Rabaul*
(CVE121), *Palau* (CVE122),
Tinian (CVE123), *Bastogne*[2]
(CVE124), *Eniwetok*[2]
(CVE125), *Lingayen*[2]

(CVE126), *Okinawa*[2]
(CVE127), CVE128-139[2]

ROYAL NAVY

Unicorn[3]

Audacious class:	*Audacious, Africa, Eagle, Irresistible*
Gibraltar class:	*Gibraltar, Malta, New Zealand*
Colossus class:	*Colossus, Perseus, Glory, Pioneer, Ocean, Theseus, Triumph, Venerable, Vengeance, Warrior*
Majestic class:	*Majestic, Magnificent, Powerful, Terrible, Hercules, Leviathan*
Hermes class:	*Hermes, Albion, Arrogant, Bulwark, Centaur, Elephant, Monmouth, Polyphemus*
Archer class:	*Archer, Avenger, Biter, Charger, Dasher*
Attacker class:	*Attacker* (ex-USS *Barnes*), *Battler* (ex-USS *Altamaha*), *Chaser* (ex-USS *Breton*), *Fencer* (ex-USS *Croatan*), *Pursuer* (ex-USS *St George*), *Stalker* (ex-USS *Hamlin*), *Striker* (ex-USS *Prince William*), *Hunter* (ex-Trailer, ex-USS *Block Island*)
Ruler class:	*Ravager, Trumpeter* (ex-USS *Bastian*), *Patroller* (ex-USS *Keeweenaw*), *Puncher* (ex-USS *Willapa*), *Reaper* (ex-USS *Winjah*), *Searcher,*

Slinger (ex-USS Chatham), Smiter (ex-USS Vermilion), Speaker (ex-USS Delgada), Tracker, Trouncer (ex-USS Perdido), Arbiter (ex-USS St Simon), Ameer (ex-USS Baffins), Atheling (ex-USS Glacier), Begum (ex-USS Balinas), Emperor (ex-USS Pybus), Empress (ex-USS Carnegie), Khedive (ex-USS Cordova), Nabob[4] (ex-USS Edisto), Premier (ex-USS Estero), Queen (ex-USS St Andrews), Rajah (ex-Prince, ex-USS McClure), Ruler (ex-USS St Joseph), Ranee (ex-USS Niantic), Shah (ex-USS Jamaica), Thane (ex-USS Sunset)

Mac-ships:

Empire MacAlpine, Empire MacKendrick, Empire MacAndrew, Empire MacDermott, Empire MacRae, Empire MacCallum (grain carriers); Empire Mackay, Empire MacColl, Empire MacMahon, Empire MacCabe, Acavus, Adula, Alexia, Amastra, Ancylus, Gadila, Macoma, Miralda, Rapana (oil tankers)

Vindex class:

Vindex, Nairana

Activity
Campania
Pretoria Castle

JAPAN

Chuyo class[5]:

Chuyo (ex-Nitta Maru), Taiyo (ex-Kasuga Maru), Unyo (ex-Yawata Maru)

Hiyo class[5]:

Hiyo (ex-Idzumo Maru), Junyo (ex-Kashiwara Maru)

Taiho + 7 cancelled
Ryuho (ex-Taigei[6])

Ocean-liner conversions:

Shinyo (ex-Scharnhorst), Kaiyo (ex-Argentina Maru) + 1 sunk before conversion

Chitose class[7]:

Chitose, Chiyoda

Ex-battleship:

Shinano

Unryu class:

Amagi, Aso, Ikoma, Kasagi, Katsuragi, Unryu

Ex-cruiser:

Ibuki

Ex-oil tankers:

Chigusa Maru, Yamashio Maru, Otakisan Maru, Shimane Maru + 2 cancelled

GERMANY

Heavy cruiser conversion:

Seydlitz

ITALY

Ocean-liner conversions:

Aquila (ex-Roma), Sparviero (ex-Falco, ex-Augustus)

Notes
[1] Second carrier of that name
[2] Cancelled
[3] Ordered as aircraft repair ship but used as escort carrier
[4] Operated by Royal Canadian Navy
[5] Converted from ocean liner
[6] Ex-submarine tenders
[7] Ex-seaplane tenders

APPENDIX 4

Typical Air Groups for World War II CVs

USS *Yorktown* (CV6) in June 1942 with Task Group 17.5 at Midway	Air Group 3: VF-3: 25 F4F Wildcats; VB-3: 18 SBD-3 Dauntlesses; VT-3: 13 TBD-1 Devastators; VS-5: 19 SBD-3 Dauntlesses *(75 aircraft in total)*
USS *Independence* (CVL22) in October-December 1943 with Task Group 38.2	Air Group 22: VF-6: 12 F6F Hellcats; VF-22: 16 F6F Hellcats; VC-22: 9 TBF Avengers *(37 aircraft in total)*
USS *Essex* (CV9) in October 1944 with Task Group 38.3 at Leyte Gulf	Air Group 15: VF-15: 45 F6F Hellcats, 4 F6F-3N Hellcats, 2 F6F-3P Hellcats; VB-15: 25 SB2C Helldivers; VT-15: 10 TBF/TBM Avengers *(96 aircraft in total)*

APPENDIX 5

Aircraft Carrier Losses 1939-1945

ROYAL NAVY

HMS *Courageous*	Torpedoed by U-29, 17 September 1939
HMS *Glorious*	Sunk by gunfire of *Scharnhorst* and *Gneisenau*, 8 June 1940
HMS *Ark Royal*	Torpedoed by *U-81*, 14 November 1941
HMS *Hermes*	Sunk by air attack, 9 April 1942
HMS *Eagle*	Torpedoed by *U-93*, 11 August 1942
HMS *Avenger*	Torpedoed by *U-155*, 15 November 1942
HMS *Dasher*	Sunk by a gas explosion, 27 March 1943
HMCS *Nabob*	Damaged beyond repair after being torpedoed by U-boat, 22 August 1944
HMS *Thane*	Damaged beyond repair after being torpedoed by U-boat, 15 January 1945

US NAVY

USS *Lexington* (CV2)	Torpedoed and bombed, 8 May 1942
USS *Yorktown* (CV5)	Torpedoed by *I-168* and bombed, 7 June 1942
USS *Wasp* (CV7)	Torpedoed by *I-19*, 15 September 1942
USS *Hornet* (CV8)	Torpedoed, 26 October 1942
USS *Liscombe Bay* (CVE56)	Torpedoed by *I-175*, 24 November 1943
USS *Block Island* (CVE21)	Torpedoed by *U-549*, 29 May 1944
USS Princeton (CVL23)	Sunk by bomb, 24 October 1944
USS *St Lô* (CVE63)	Sunk by kamikaze, 25 October 1944
USS *Gambier Bay* (CVE73)	Sunk by gunfire, 25 October 1944
USS *Ommaney Bay* (CVE79)	Sunk by kamikaze, 4 January 1945
USS *Bismarck Sea* (CVE95)	Sunk by kamikaze, 21 February 1945

JAPAN

Shoho	Sunk by air attack, 8 May 1942
Akagi	Sunk by bombs, 4 June 1942
Kaga	Sunk by bombs, 4 June 1942
Hiryu	Sunk by bombs, 4 June 1942
Soryu	Sunk by bombs, 4 June 1942
Ryujo	Sunk by air attack, 24 August 1942
Chuyo	Torpedoed by *Sailfish*, 4 December 1943
Shokaku	Torpedoed by *Cavalla*, 19 June 1944
Taiho	Torpedoed by *Albacore*, 19 June 1944
Hiyo	Sunk by air attack, 20 June 1944
Taiyo	Torpedoed by *Rasher*, 18 August 1944
Unyo	Torpedoed by *Barb*, 16 September 1944
Zuikaku	Sunk by air attack, 25 October 1944
Zuiho	Sunk by air attack, 25 October 1944
Chitose	Sunk by air attack, 25 October 1944
Chiyoda	Sunk by air attack, 25 October 1944
Shinyo	Torpedoed by *Spadefish*, 17 November 1944
Shinano	Torpedoed by *Archerfish*, 29 November 1944
Unryu	Torpedoed by *Redfish*, 19 December 1944
Yamashio Maru	Sunk by air attack, 17 February 1945
Amagi	Sunk by air attack, 24 July 1945
Shimane Maru	Sunk by air attack, 24 July 1945
Otakisan Maru	Mined, 25 August 1945

APPENDIX 6

Aircraft Carriers Ordered 1946-1999

Name (No.)	Authorized	Fate
United States[1] (CVB58)	FY '48	Cancelled 1949
Forrestal[2] (CVA59)	FY '52	Stricken 1993
Saratoga (CVA60)	FY '53	Stricken 1994
Ranger (CVA61)	FY '54	Stricken 1993
Independence (CVA62)	FY '55	Stricken 1999
Kitty Hawk (CVA63)	FY '56	In service 1999
Constellation (CVA64)	FY '57	In service 1999
America (CVA66)	FY '61	Stricken 1996
John F Kennedy (CVA67)	FY '63	In service 1999
Enterprise (CVAN65)	FY '58	In service 1999
Nimitz (CVAN68)	FY '67	In service 1999
Dwight D Eisenhower (CVN69)	FY '70	In service 1999
Carl Vinson (CVN70)	FY '74	In service 1999
Theodore Roosevelt (CVN71)	FY '80	In service 1999
Abraham Lincoln (CVN72)	FY '83	In service 1999
George Washington (CVN73)	FY '83	In service 1999
John C Stennis (CVN74)	FY '88	In service 1999
Harry S Truman (CVN75)	FY '88	In service 1999
Ronald Reagan (CVN76)	FY '94	Building
CVN77	FY '99	Projected

Notes

[1] Designation would have changed to CVA (attack carrier)
[2] All CVAs reclassified as CVs in 1975

APPENDIX 7

US Aircraft Carriers in Service Worldwide 1946-1999

US NAVY

Enterprise (CV6) In reserve 1947; stricken 1956

Essex (CV9) Modernized 1948-51; in reserve 1969; stricken 1973

Yorktown (CV10) Modernized 1951-53; stricken 1973

Intrepid (CV11) Modernized 1951-54; stricken 1973

Hornet (CV12) Modernized 1951-53; in reserve 1979; stricken 1989

Franklin (CV13) In reserve 1946; stricken 1964

Ticonderoga (CV14) Modernized 1951-54; stricken 1973

Randolph (CV15) Modernized 1951-53; in reserve 1969; stricken 1973

Lexington (CV16) Modernized 1952-55; training 1983; stricken 1991

Bunker Hill (CV17) Laid up 1947; used for trials and stricken 1966

Wasp (CV18) Modernised 1948-51; in reserve 1970; stricken 1972

Hancock (CV19) Modernized 1951-54; stricken 1976

Bennington (CV20) Modernized 1950-52; in reserve 1970; stricken 1989

Boxer (CV21) Converted to assault helicopter carrier 1959 and redesignated LPH4; stricken 1969

Belleau Wood (CVL24) Transferred to France as *Bois Belleau* 1953; returned and stricken 1960

Cowpens (CVL25) In reserve 1947; stricken 1959

Monterey (CVL26) Training 1951-55; in reserve 1956; stricken 1970

Langley (CVL27) Transferred to France as *Lafayette* 1951; returned and stricken 1963

Cabot (CVL28) Training and ASW 1948-55; transferred to Spain as *Dédalo* 1967; returned and preserved 1989

Bataan (CVL29) Aircraft transport 1950-53; in reserve 1954; stricken 1959

San Jacinto (CVL30) In reserve 1947; stricken 1970

Bon Homme
Richard (CV31)   Modernized 1952-55;
                   in reserve 1971;
                   stricken 1989

Leyte (CV32)   Training 1946-50;
                   in reserve 1959;
                   stricken 1969

Kearsarge (CV33)   Modernized 1950-52;
                   in reserve 1970;
                   stricken 1973

Oriskany (CV34)   In reserve 1970;
                   stricken 1989

Antietam (CV36)   Angled-deck conversion
                   1952; in reserve 1963;
                   stricken 1973

Princeton (CV37)   Converted to assault
                   helicopter carrier and
                   redesignated LPH-5;
                   stricken 1970

Shangri-la (CV38) Modernized 1951-55;
                   in reserve 1971;
                   stricken 1982

Lake Champlain
(CV39)   Modernized 1950-52;
                   in reserve 1966;
                   stricken 1969

Tarawa (CV40)   In reserve 1960;
                   stricken 1967

Midway (CVB41)   Stricken 1993

Franklin D Roosevelt
(CVB42)   Stricken 1977

Coral Sea (CVB43) Stricken 1990

Valley Forge (CV45) Converted to assault
                     helicopter carrier 1961 and
                     redesignated LPH-8;
                     stricken 1970

Philippine Sea
(CV47)   In reserve 1958;
                   stricken 1969

Saipan (CVL48)   Converted to command ship
                   1963-64 and renamed
                   Arlington (AGMR-2);
                   stricken 1975

Wright (CVL49)   Converted to command ship
                   and redesignated CC-3;
                   in reserve 1970;
                   stricken 1977

AMPHIBIOUS-ASSAULT HELICOPTER CARRIERS

Block Island
(LPH1)
(ex-CVE106)   Conversion cancelled 1955

Iwo Jima (LPH2)   New construction FY 1958;
                   stricken 1993

Okinawa (LPH3)   New construction FY 1959;
                   stricken 1993

Boxer (LPH4)
(ex-CVS21)
Ex-CVA (1959);   Stricken 1969

Princeton (LPH5)
(ex-CVS37)
Ex-CVA (1959);   Stricken 1970

Thetis Bay (LPH6)
(ex-CVE90)   Conversion 1956;
                   stricken 1966

Guadalcanal (LPH7)	New construction FY 1960; stricken 1994	*Tripoli* (LPH10)	New construction FY 1963; stricken 1995
Valley Forge (LPH8) (ex-CVS45) Ex-CVA (1961)	Stricken 1970	*New Orleans* (LPH11)	New construction FY 1965; stricken 1997
Guam (LPH9)	New construction FY 1962; stricken 1998	*Inchon* (LPH12)	New construction FY 1966; conversion to MCM support ship MCS-12 1996

Above: The *Admiral Kuznetzov* was launched in 1985, and her name recalls the Soviet admiral most closely identified with carriers and an integrated blue-water fleet. She was still unfinished at Nikolayev when the Soviet Union broke up, and as of 1992 her fate was uncertain. Admiral Kuznetzov slipped into the Mediterranean in December 1991 for the trip home to the Northern Fleet. She was still incomplete in mid-1992 with many of her antennae not connected to any internal electronics. Compared to the earlier *Kiev* class, these ships presumably represent a shift in Soviet policy. From the mid-1970s on, Admiral Gorshkov advertised the Soviet Navy as a 'sure shield' against Western intervention in 'wars of national liberation' in the Third World, i.e. against US carrier battle groups. But as planning for this projected proceeded, Soviet comments about carrier operations became markedly more respectful. As of early 1992, Kuznetzov had experienced relatively little air activity, and it appeared that only a few pilots had been carrier-qualified. She has operated Su-27 Flanker, MiG-29 Fulcrum and Su-25 Frogfoot aircraft. All aircraft are normally stowed below decks in a closed hangar. Hangar length is limited by the unusual (for a carrier) nest of SS-N-19 missiles under the flight deck, in launching tubes. The Punch Bowl satellite link serves these SS-N-19s.

APPENDIX 8

The Russian (ex-Soviet) Navy's Carrier *Admiral Kuznetsov*

Displacement:
45,900 tons (standard), 58,500 tons (full load)

Dimensions:
999ft (overall), 916ft 6in (waterline) x 229ft 9in (overall) x 34ft 1in
304.5m, 280m x 70.37m x 10.5m

Machinery:
4-shaft steam turbines, 200,000 horsepower

Speed:
30 knots

Range:
3850 nautical miles at full speed; 8500nm at 18 knots

Armament:
12 Granit 4K-80 anti-ship missiles
4 Klinok surface-to-air missile systems
8 Kortik/Kashtan missile/gun air defence systems
6 AK-630 Gatling close-in weapon systems
2 RBU-1200 anti-submarine rocket-launchers

Aircraft:
18 Su-27K/Su-33 Flanker-Ds
4 Su-25 UTG Frogfoots
15 Ka-27 Helix anti-submarine helicopters
2 Ka-31 RLD airborne early warning (AEW) helicopters

Sensors:
Radar Sky Watch
2 Strut Pair
3 Palm Frond
1 Plate Steer
3 Cross Sword (FCS)
Sonar LF hull
2 Punch Bowl satellite antennas

APPENDIX 9

Fixed-wing Aircraft Carriers in Service Worldwide in 1999

US NAVY

USS *Kitty Hawk*
(CV63)   Commissioned
                          1961

USS *Constellation*
(CV64)   Commissioned
                          1961

USS *Enterprise*
(CVN65)   Commissioned
                          1961

USS *John F Kennedy*
(CV66)   Commissioned
                          1968

USS *Nimitz* (CVN68)   Commissioned
                          1975

USS *Dwight D Eisenhower*
(CVN69)   Commissioned
                          1977

USS *Carl Vinson*
(CVN70)   Commissioned
                          1982

USS *Theodore Roosevelt*
(CVN71)   Commissioned
                          1986

USS *Abraham Lincoln*
(CVN72)   Commissioned
                          1989

USS *George Washington*
(CVN73)   Commissioned
                          1992

USS *John C Stennis*
(CVN74)   Commissioned
                          1995

USS *Harry S Truman*
(CVN75)   Commissioned
                          1998

Ronald Reagan (CVN76)   To be
                          commissioned 2002

CVN77   Projected for
                          completion in 2008

ROYAL NAVY

HMS *Invincible*   Commissioned
                          1980

HMS *Illustrious*   Commissioned
                          1982

HMS *Ark Royal*
(ex-*Indomitable*)   Commissioned
                          1985

2 CV(F)   Projected

RUSSIA

Admiral Kuznetsov   Commissioned
                          1991

FRANCE

Charles de Gaulle   On trials; to be
                          commissioned 2002

Foch   Commissioned 1963

+ 1 CV/CVN — Projected

+ 2 — To be decommissioned 2001

BRAZIL

BNS *Minas Gerais* — Commissioned 1945

ITALY

Giuseppe Garibaldi — Commissioned 1985

+ 1 NUM[1] — Projected

SPAIN

Principe de Asturias — Commissioned 1988

THAILAND

HTMS *Chakkrinareubet* — Commissioned 1997

Above: HMS *Illustrious*, second of the *Invincible-class* carriers. Originally planned as a helicopter-carrying cruiser, the development of the Sea Harrier meant that this class could operate STOVL aircraft. The more powerful engine, more fuel and new avionics provided the pilot with computer-aided navigation and attack data. While *Invincible* was under construction a very simple improvement was perfected which revolutionized flying at sea. This is the 'ski-jump' ramp which gives the Sea Harrier sufficient lift to take off using less fuel or carrying more payload.

Note

[1] Nouva Unitá Maggiore = New Major Unit

APPENDIX 10

Helicopter Carriers in Service Worldwide in 1999

US NAVY

USS *Tarawa*
(LHA1)   Commissioned 1976[1]

USS *Saipan* (LHA1)   Commissioned 1977[1]

USS *Belleau Wood*
(LHA3)   Commissioned 1978[1]

USS *Nassau* (LHA4)
                         Commissioned 1979[1]

USS *Peleliu*
(LHA5, ex-Da Nang)   Commissioned 1980[1]

USS *Wasp* (LHD1)
                         Commissioned 1989[1]

USS *Essex* (LHD2)
                         Commissioned 1992[1]

USS *Kearsarge* (LHD3)
                         Commissioned 1993[1]

USS *Boxer* (LHD4)
                         Commissioned 1995[1]

USS *Bataan* (LHD5)
                         Commissioned 1997[1]

USS *Bon Homme Richard*
(LHD6)   Commissioned 1998[1]

+ *Iwo Jima* (LHD7)   Building

+LHD8   Projected

Note
[1]LHAs and LHDs carry variable air groups of helicopters
and STOVL support aircraft

ROYAL NAVY

HMS Ocean   Commissioned 1998

A number of navies also operate amphibious ships with a limited air capability (usually helicopters, but sometimes STOVL aircraft on a temporary basis). Japan's Maritime Self Defence Force operates four large helicopter-carrying destroyers (DDHs), embarking three SH-60J Seahawk anti-submarine helicopters, but in other the large surface warships of other navies two helicopters is usually the maximum.

Index

Page references in *italics* refer to illustrations.

PICTURE CREDITS
All artworks: Istituto Geografico De Agostini
All photographs TRH Pictures except the following:
Hugh Cowin: 136, 137